# BUSHCRAFT AND WILDERNESS SURVIVAL SKILLS FOR KIDS

GUIDE TO FOSTER PROBLEM-SOLVING ABILITIES AND CRITICAL THINKING WHILE LEARNING HOW TO START A FIRE, UNDERSTAND THE WEATHER, BUILD SHELTERS, PERFORM FIRST AID AND MORE.

CONRAD PRESLEY

© **Copyright 2023 Unlimited Concepts. All rights reserved.**

The content contained within this book may not be reproduced, duplicated, or transmitted without direct written permission from the author or the publisher.

Under no circumstances will any blame or legal responsibility be held against the publisher or author for any damages, reparation, or monetary loss due to the information contained within this book. Either directly or indirectly. You are responsible for your own choices, actions, and results.

**Legal Notice:**

This book is copyright-protected. This book is only for personal use. You cannot amend, distribute, sell, use, quote, or paraphrase any part, or the content within this book, without the consent of the author or publisher.

**Disclaimer Notice:**

Please note the information contained within this document is for educational and entertainment purposes only. All effort has been executed to present accurate, up-to-date, reliable, and complete information. No warranties of any kind are declared or implied. Readers acknowledge the author is not engaged in rendering legal, financial, medical, or professional advice. The content within this book has been derived from various sources. Please consult a licensed professional before attempting any techniques outlined in this book.

By reading this document, the reader agrees that under no circumstances is the author or publisher responsible for any losses, direct or indirect, which are incurred as a result of the use of the information contained within this document, including, but not limited to errors, omissions, or inaccuracies.

For permissions requests, speaking inquiries, and bulk order purchase options, email: publishing@uconcept.com.

ISBN: 978-1-960188-24-3 | E-book

ISBN: 978-1-960188-27-4 | Paperback

ISBN: 978-1-960188-28-1 | Hardcover

Published by Unlimited Concepts, Coconut Creek, Florida.

www.publishing.uconcept.com

Book, Editing, and Cover Design by Janet M Garcia | UConceptDesigns.com

Published in the United States of America.

*To my family*

*With gratitude to my family and especially to my son for all the years we spent together in the wild exploring and enjoying nature.*

# LEAVE A 1-CLICK REVIEW

I would be incredibly thankful if you take just
60-seconds to write a brief review on Amazon,
even if it's just a few sentences!

https://amazon.com/review/create-review?asin=1960188275

# INTRODUCTION

Have you ever imagined what it'd be like for you to live in a bush, like a little bunny? It'd be fun if only you knew how to survive there. And this is where bushcraft skills come in.

Before we go into what bushcraft is, let's go back in history. Do you know that for 95 percent of our time on earth, humans have survived by hunting and gathering food from the natural environment? These men of ancient times often lived in caves or bushes. To survive, they had to use their imagination to find food in their natural environment. In fact, this is what humans (or *homo sapiens*) have been doing since we appeared around 200,000 years ago till about 11,000 years ago when we started developing agriculture.

In essence, humans foraged for food while they lived in the bush. In case you're wondering, *foraging* means relying on food that nature provides through what plants and, small animals, insects, and birds have gathered. Also, when humans or animals forage, they rely on other scavenging animals killed by predators and on

# INTRODUCTION

hunting. So, when you hear the word foraging, think of the term "*hunting-gathering*" because you can use them interchangeably.

As we lived in the bush foraging wild, we learned to hunt and gather, and developed other essential abilities to survive the harsh conditions of the bushes. While this might have been tough, there are many people today who consider this activity fun. These people go into the wilderness and woodlands to reconnect with the world of nature and learn some ancient survival skills. We aren't just talking about foraging here but *bushcraft*.

But what exactly is bushcraft? In the simplest terms, bushcraft is the skills you need to live and survive in the bush. But I don't mean just any kind of bush. I mean a part of the country that is wild, remote, and generally has no one living around there. Sounds scary, right? But you can do this.

Living in the bush may not be as much of a big deal as it may sound. For example, building shelter, fire, and finding water and food may be everything you need to survive there. All you need to do is learn how to do it. While they are essential, they're just the minimum requirements since they only help you to survive rather than to live. Think about it like this. You live in a house where you can bathe, eat and drink water. In this case, you are simply surviving. The skills you need will go beyond these because living is more than just being able to survive. So, you must have skills that extend beyond these basic things, and this is what bushcraft teaches you.

## SURVIVAL SKILLS OR BUSHCRAFT?

Have you heard of survival skills? It's possible to use them as synonyms of each other because they sort of overlap in the skills required. Technically, they have a lot in common. But what could that be? Stay with me. Probably the only difference between both of them is the situation and reason why they are applied.

For example, when you hear the word "*survival*" from adults on TV or your favorite kiddies' YouTube channel, it's probably used to refer to surviving natural disasters, accidents, plane crashes, or war. You can also use it in a military situation to escape an enemy trying to attack you. In fact, you can relate it to a word called "*preppers*," which is like preparing for an imminent threat by, let's say, stockpiling food and other kinds of supplies. All of these still refer to *survival*.

In contrast, *bushcraft*, is more about enjoying the experience of living in a remote, wild location. You aren't expecting an army to attack you, a natural disaster to occur, or something bad to happen to you. So you're doing more than just surviving. You are simply trying to live life outdoors and appreciate nature's beauty and uniqueness.

People in survival situations are trying to return to civilization safely and as soon as possible. But those doing bushcraft aren't in a hurry since they're happy to make a comfortable home in the wild.

## LEARNING SOME COMMON SKILLS

No matter the situation you find yourself in, you will need some of these common skills. Yes, everyone should learn some skills to stay safe and survive in the wild. These are some important skills:

- Using tools like a saw and knife safely.

## INTRODUCTION

- Making a fire and keeping it burning using different methods.
- Building a shelter using natural or man-made things.
- Finding, filtering, and cleaning water to make it safe to drink.
- Finding food like plants and wild animals and cooking them on a fire.
- Finding your way using a compass, the sun, stars, and other natural things.
- Knowing how to take care of yourself or others if you get hurt or sick.

The skills you need may change depending on where you are and what you have with you. For example, you might need to make a knife from a rock or find water in a desert. You also need to be aware of any risks and how to stay safe. You can also consider some of these situations:

- How will you start a fire?
- Do you have a lighter or matches, or will you need to use sticks to create a fire?
- Will you use a tent to shelter, or will you build it from natural things like sticks and leaves?
- Depending on where you are, it may be hard to find water or food, so you need to be careful and have a plan.
- Will you stay in one place or walk around to find things?

Finally, it's important to be careful of your surroundings, like the land, plants, and animals, and know how to treat any injuries or sicknesses that might happen.

INTRODUCTION

ARE THERE SOME DIFFERENCES?

If you're planning a trip to the wild, in addition to having an adult around, you will probably need items that make life comfortable in the wild. Also, you will need a rucksack containing essential items such as a knife, fire-steel, tarpaulin, and billycan. But someone in a survival situation may not need all of these as they won't be so lucky. They could have only a survival tin even though their security would be better. Also, they may need to improvise more to survive.

As someone who wants to engage in bushcraft, you may be interested in learning about natural history and understanding the earth's flora and fauna better. Similarly, someone preparing for a survival situation also needs to understand their natural environment to help them deal with danger more efficiently.

Imagine you are in a place where there are many plants with fruits that look good to eat, but not all of them are safe. Or imagine you are near the sea, but you don't know which sea animals are good to eat. It is important to know which ones are good to eat so that you can have a tasty and healthy meal without getting sick.

If you ever find yourself lost in the wild, it's important to know how to ask for help. You might need someone to rescue you or your group. So, what can you do to attract help? Will you try to stay in one place and make yourself visible, or will you try to move to a more visible location? Also, are you going to try to find your way to safety? These are important things to know if you're exploring the wild and are very important in a survival situation.

People who like to do bushcraft learn skills to survive in the wild. They learn how to use tools like knives and saws, make a fire, build a shelter, find clean water and food, and know how to find

INTRODUCTION

their way around. But sometimes, they also like to make things like clothes or cups from natural materials. However, if they are in a survival situation, they may not have time to do those things. Making a bow and arrow might seem like a good idea, but it takes a lot of time and practice. So, it's important to focus on the survival skills first.

HOW IS THIS DIFFERENT FROM CAMPING?

Some people might think that bushcraft is just like camping. But bushcraft is a special kind of camping that teaches you how to survive and live in the wild using only natural materials and tools. It's like going back in time to the days when people made everything they needed from the things around them. You learn how to build your own shelter, start a fire without matches, find your own food and water, and use the stars to navigate. So, bushcraft is a lot like camping, but with some really cool and useful skills you can learn!

Also, when we go camping, we usually take a lot of modern equipment with us. But sometimes, it's fun to try and make things ourselves using materials we find in nature. This is what makes bushcraft special! We can still enjoy being outside in nature even if we can't have a campfire. We can use a stove instead. Also, camping gear has become lighter and easier to carry, which is really helpful when we go on long hikes or walks.

In summary, *camping* is like being outside. Still, *bushcraft* is more about learning how to live and do things in nature, about using natural tools to explore and navigate. It's like having an adventure and learning new skills at the same time!

Finally, I'd love to welcome you, young explorers! In this book on bushcraft, you will learn a variety of essential skills to help you survive and thrive in the great outdoors. From building shelters and navigating the wilderness to foraging for food and mastering fire creation, this book will equip you with the tools and knowledge you need to connect with nature and have fun exploring. So, get ready to embark on an exciting adventure and discover the wonders of bushcraft!

# BUSHCRAFT BASICS FOR YOUNG EXPLORERS

## What is Bushcraft?

Most of us live in cities and have everything we need at our fingertips - food, water, heat, and shelter. But if we were outside in nature, we might not know how to take care of ourselves. Bushcraft is about learning how to survive in the wild by using some important survival skills and knowing how to take care of yourself if you get hurt. It's like going back to basics and learning how to live using what nature provides.

When we hear the word *bushcraft*, we might think of a person who is an expert in surviving in the wild. But bushcraft is simply a set of skills and knowledge that can help us survive in the outdoors. For example, building a shelter, making a fire, and finding food and water are all essential bushcraft skills. Bushcraft also includes other skills like making ropes, identifying plants, and understanding natural ways to navigate. It's an area of knowledge that even some people studying in universities have trouble understanding fully, as a bushcraft expert named Lizzy Maskey said.

Another way to understand bushcraft is this: we enjoy spending time outside; we start looking at things around us and become curious about how we can use them. We try to learn more about the natural world and how everything is connected. For example, if we want to find owls, we can look for signs of mice and voles, as they are the prey for owls. It's like putting together a puzzle!

Remember that bushcraft isn't just about surviving. Survival means knowing *how* to stay alive in different situations, while bushcraft is about using nature to your advantage. With bushcraft, you learn how to work with and use the things around you instead of just chopping them down. So, like I said above, it's like solving a puzzle with the help of nature.

Learning bushcraft skills can help us develop important qualities like patience, perseverance, humility, observation, and resilience. It makes us feel more confident, independent, and less dependent on others. In the past, people had to know how to start a fire by rubbing sticks together and which plants have medicinal properties to survive, but now we have modern tools and technology that make life easier. However, it's still important to learn these basic human skills that have kept us alive for thousands of years.

## ESSENTIAL BUSHCRAFT SKILLS

Some people think that bushcraft skills are only for surviving in the wilderness. Still, they can actually make our time in the woods more comfortable and fun. These skills are also called *pioneer skills* because they were necessary for survival before we had things like electricity, cars, and toilets. Nowadays, we don't need to build fires or boil water every day. However, it's still important to learn these skills in case of an emergency or if we want to live more independently. So, let's look at some essential bushcraft skills you can learn.

## CAMPING SKILLS

Knowing how to camp can be an essential skill on its own. For instance, when you go camping in the woods, it's important to pick the right spot to set up your camp. If you pick the wrong spot, it can make things harder for you. So, you need to keep a few things in mind when choosing a spot. At first, it might feel like a lot to think about, but don't worry; with practice, it will become easier.

Let's look at what you need when choosing a camp.

- **How long are you staying?** Decide how many days you want to stay at the campsite.
- **Firewood:** Check if it's okay to have a fire and if you can cut down trees. See if there is enough deadwood to use for the fire instead.
- **Weather:** Find out which way the wind usually blows and choose a spot where the wind is parallel to your shelter and fire so that smoke doesn't blow into your shelter.
- **Elevation:** Look for a spot that is halfway up a hill between a ridge and a valley, if possible, as it will be warmer and less windy.
- **Water:** Check if there is a water source nearby, but make sure it won't flood your campsite.
- **Overhead hazards**: Check if there are any hazards like dead trees or branches overhead or cliff sides where rocks could fall into your campsite.

- **Make sure you are allowed to camp** in the area and if you need permission from the landowner or a permit. Also, check if you can have a fire, cut trees, hunt, fish, etc.

## BUSHCRAFT KNIFE SKILLS – KNIFECRAFT

Learning how to use a bushcraft belt knife is super important when you're out in the wild. If you have a good knife, you can use it to help you survive. But it's also important to know how to use it safely. Make sure to avoid cutting in the area around your upper legs and groin where there are important blood vessels. This area is called the *triangle of death*, so it's best to keep your knife away from there!

Also, this is important when using a small knife, like the ones on a pocket tool or a Swiss Army knife. When you're cutting something, make sure the blade and the direction of the cut are away from your fingers. It's like making a triangle with your fingers and keeping the knife outside of that triangle to stay safe.

- Hold the knife safely using different grips like the knee or chest lever grip.
- Use the knife to split wood to make small pieces for starting a fire.
- Cut special shapes into sticks, like a V shape or a stake shape, to help build things like a shelter or trap.
- Use the knife to make thin, curly shavings from sticks to help start a fire.
- Cut small holes in sticks to make things like a whistle or a flute.
- Use the knife to make thin, flat pieces of wood for building things like a table or a chair.

- Keep the knife sharp by sharpening it in the field or at home when it gets dull.

Also, for safety, make sure you have a sheath for your knife, especially one that you can attach to your belt. This way, you can carry it safely. Whenever you are not using your knife, make sure to put it back on the cover. This will help keep you and others around you safe.

## BUSHCRAFT AXE SKILLS – AXECRAFT

Axecraft is a fancy way of saying you know how to use a special tool called a *bushcraft axe* or *hatchet* safely. When you go camping, you need to do a lot of things with wood, like chopping it up. The bushcraft axe is great for that! It helps you get things done quickly. Below are some bushcraft axe skills.

Bushcraft axe can be used to cut down trees for firewood or to make a shelter. You can also use it to carve and shape big pieces of wood into different tools or shapes. Sometimes, you might need to use an axe as a hammer to put up a tent or to make something sturdy, like a fence. You can also sharpen an axe or replace the handle if it gets broken. Knowing these skills can make it easier to have fun and stay safe in the woods.

When you use an axe in the woods, it's really important to be safe. Cutting down a big tree with an axe can be very dangerous because the axe can swing, and the tree can fall and hurt you. Do well to learn the right way to use an axe so you don't get hurt. One way to stay safe when holding an axe is to always keep a cover on the axe head when you're not using it.

## BUSHCRAFT SAW SKILLS – SAWCRAFT

One of the most important bushcraft skills is learning how to use a saw. There are different types of saws, such as a folding saw, a bow saw, and a buck saw. It's important to choose the right size saw for the job, as using a saw that is too big can be dangerous.

Here are some important things to learn when it comes to using a saw:

- **Felling trees:** This means cutting down a tree. It is safer to use a saw for this than an axe, but you still need to be careful of the falling tree.
- **Limbing a tree:** This means cutting off the branches from a fallen tree.
- **Splitting wood:** You can use a saw to split wood, which is important for making firewood.
- **Notching logs or sticks:** This means cutting small notches into logs or sticks for building structures or making other things.
- **Processing deadfall:** This means cutting up fallen trees or branches for firewood.
- **Sharpening a saw blade:** To keep the saw working well, you need to sharpen the blade from time to time.
- **Choosing the right blade:** There are different types of saw blades for different jobs, so it's important to choose the right one for what you're cutting.

Using a saw is easier than using an axe, but there are still some important things to keep in mind. Some saws are made to cut only in one direction. If you don't know this and use the saw in the wrong way, it can cause a lot of trouble. You might get frustrated or, even worse, break the saw or hurt yourself. So, it's important to learn how to use the saw the right way to avoid any problems.

## BUSHCRAFT FIRE STARTING SKILLS – FIRECRAFT

Starting a fire in the woods is very important because it can help you stay warm, make your drinking water safe, and even call for help if you need it. But starting a fire is not as easy as it seems!

There are a lot of bushcraft skills that you need to learn before you can start a fire in the woods. These skills will also help you understand what tools you need. When you're out in the woods, you might want to make a fire to cook food or keep warm. To do that, you need to know how to start a fire safely.

Here are some things you can learn to do:

- Find and identify natural dry fire tinder (some things like dry grass, leaves, or bark make good tinder for starting fires)
- Make a "bird nest" and twig bundle to help start the fire
- Use a *Ferro rod* (a tool that creates sparks) to start the fire
- Use flint and steel (or a hard rock and your bushcraft knife or saw) to start the fire
- Build and use a bow drill (a tool that creates friction to start a fire)
- Gather and cut kindling (small sticks and twigs to add to the fire)
- Make a feather stick (a stick that has shavings cut into it to help start the fire)
- Make *char cloth* (cloth that has been turned into a type of charcoal that can help start fires)

- Start a fire with a magnifying lens (like a magnifying glass)
- Build a fire lay (a way to stack the sticks and logs to help the fire burn well)
- Choose a safe fire site (a spot where the fire won't spread or cause damage)
- Maintain a fire (add wood when needed and keep an eye on it)
- Extinguish a fire properly (make sure the fire is completely out before you leave it, using water or dirt to put it out)

Learning these things can be fun and helpful, but always make sure you're being safe and responsible when starting a fire. Also, it's important to be careful when starting a fire outside. Some places have rules about when and where you can start a fire, and it's important to follow them. If you start a fire in a place where it's not allowed, you can get in trouble. So, before you start a fire, make sure it's okay to do so in your area.

## BUSHCRAFT SHELTER BUILDING SKILLS – SHELTERCRAFT

To have a comfy sleep in the woods, you need something to sleep on, in, and under. Building a bushcraft shelter can be super fun, but it depends on how long you're planning to stay and if you're allowed to build one where you are. If you can't build a shelter, you can use a bushcraft tent or a tarp. Hammocks are great, too, especially if the ground is not flat. And if you're in an emergency, you can use a survival blanket, a tarp, and a *bivy bag* to stay warm.

Here are some exciting things you can learn to do when building a shelter:

- Make a special type of cloth that's waterproof and can be used to make a tent
- Set up a tarp in different ways to create a shelter
- Make a rope that goes from one tree to another and can hold up a tarp
- Create your own stakes to hold down your tent or tarp
- Make a comfortable place to sleep by crafting a pad or mattress
- Build a shelter from branches called a *lean-to*
- Make a shelter called a *debris hut* out of things you find on the ground
- Build an *A-Frame* shelter using poles
- Create a raised bed inside your shelter to keep you off the ground
- Make a safe way to heat your shelter
- Find materials in nature to help keep you warm and dry
- Build a wall to keep heat from a fire close to your shelter

## WATER SOURCING AND PURIFICATION SKILLS

Having clean drinking water is extremely important for our survival. We need water not just for drinking but also for cooking, cleaning utensils, and keeping ourselves clean. When we go out into the woods, we need to make sure we have a plan to get clean water to drink. It's important to remember that most natural water has tiny living organisms in it that can make us sick. Even if a stream looks clear, it might not be safe to drink from.

Here are some skills you can learn to make sure you have clean water while you're out in the woods:

- **Finding a water source:** Learn how to locate water sources like streams, rivers, and lakes.
- **Judging the safety of water:** Figure out if the water is safe to drink by looking for signs of pollution or contamination.
- **Choosing the right container:** Make sure you have a container that's safe for carrying water and won't leak.
- **Picking the right pot:** Choose a pot that's good for boiling water over a fire.
- **Building a pot hanger:** Construct a hanger to hold your pot over the fire.
- **Filtering the water:** Use a coarse filter to get rid of dirt and debris before boiling or filtering the water.
- **Boiling the water:** Boil the water to kill any harmful bacteria or viruses.
- **Using a water filter:** Use a water filter to remove impurities from the water, and make sure you know how to use and clean it properly.
- **Identifying water indicator trees:** Learn how to spot certain trees that can indicate the presence of water.
- **Collecting water from birch trees:** Learn how to collect water from birch trees by tapping into the sap.
- **Building a multilevel tripod water filter:** Build a water filter using natural materials like rocks, sand, and charcoal to purify water.

It's always important to have a metal container to clean water when you're out in nature. Having two containers is even better:

one to clean water and one to store it so it stays clean. This way, you can make sure you don't mix dirty water with clean water.

To clean water quickly, I use a special tool called a *Grayl Geopress water filter*, and I pair it with a cup that can also be used to hold food. This way, I have everything I need to stay safe and hydrated while I'm exploring nature.

## BUSHCRAFT CORDAGE SKILLS – BINDCRAFT

*Bindcraft* is a very important skill that includes making ropes from natural materials like plants or using man-made ropes like paracord. Learning how to tie different kinds of knots with these ropes can help you in many ways in the woods. For instance, you can use them to build a shelter, to do first aid, or to make tools. Knowing how to tie the right knots can make your life much easier and safer in the wild.

If you're interested in bindcraft, here are some skills you can practice with cordage:

- Choosing the right type of cordage, like paracord or bank line, for different tasks.
- Learning to identify natural materials that can be used to make cordage, like plant fibers or animal tendons.
- Weaving and braiding these materials into strong cordage that can be used for a variety of purposes.
- Mastering basic knots, like the square knot and the bowline, that are essential in bindcraft.
- Learning how to tie lashings, which are useful for building structures like shelters or tripods.
- Making bindings that can be used for securing things like arrowheads or other tools.

- Creating fish nets that can be used for catching food in a survival situation.
- Cordage can be made from rawhide, which can be used for a variety of tasks.
- Make and use toggles, which are like little buttons that can be used to fasten things together. They can be made from bone, wood, or other materials and are great for securing things like bags or clothing.

Here are some **easy-to-learn knots** that can be helpful when you're camping:

- **Lark's Head:** a knot used to attach a rope to an object
- **Stop Knot:** a simple knot used to keep the rope from slipping through an object
- **Marline Spike Hitch:** a knot used to tie a rope to a spike or pole
- **Prusik Knot:** a knot used to attach a smaller rope to a larger rope
- **Jam Knot:** a knot used to hold two ropes together tightly
- **Half Hitch:** a simple knot used to secure a rope to an object
- **Fisherman's Knot:** a knot used to join two ropes together
- **Reef Knot:** a knot used to tie two ends of a rope together
- **Bowline:** a knot used to make a loop at the end of a rope
- **Trucker's Hitch:** a knot used to secure a load to a vehicle
- **Clove Hitch:** a knot used to attach a rope to an object
- **Timber Hitch:** a knot used to attach a rope to a log or other round object
- **Slip Knot:** a knot that can be easily untied by pulling one end

You might think that all knots are the same, but some of them, like the prusik knot, are really amazing. You can use just two pieces of rope to pitch a tent or climb a mountain without even untying the knot. It's so simple yet so useful!

To get good at tying knots, I keep a piece of strong rope and thin string next to my chair and practice tying knots. If I don't practice, I'll forget how to do them.

## TOOLS OF THE TRADE: BUSHCRAFT ESSENTIALS

We often get asked what are the must-have things for bushcraft. It's not an easy question to answer because everyone has their own preferences. Depending on where you're going, how long you'll be there, and who you're going with, your needs can vary. But we are up for the challenge. Although, remember that it's not a strict list that you have to follow. Here are the 14 things that you'll need for bushcraft:

## BLADE

A blade is a really useful tool to have when you're out in the woods. It's a strong and versatile tool that can be used for lots of different tasks. You can use it to make a shelter, hunt, cook, clear things out of the way, and even make other tools or objects. So, it's a really important tool to have with you. There are two types of blades you might want to consider adding to your bushcraft gear.

- **Fallkniven F1** – The Fallkniven F1 is an awesome knife that is perfect for bushcraft. It's really strong but also very light, which makes it easy to use. If you're looking

for a new knife for the first time or need to replace your old one, this is definitely one to consider!
- **Kershaw Camp 10 Machete** – The Kershaw Camp 10 Machete is a really cool tool that can help you get your job done super fast. It's strong and balanced, which means you can use it to do even the toughest tasks really easily. We love it because it's not too expensive and it works really well. It's like having a superhero on your side when you need to get things done outside.

## WATER PURIFICATION

Talking about water purification can be a little tricky because it depends on what you like and how long you'll be outside. If you're going to be outside for a short time, it's a good idea to carry a water bottle with a filter. But if you're going to be outside for a long time and don't have much space, you might want to carry purification pens or tablets instead. There's no right or wrong choice; just make sure you think about how long you'll be outside and how much space you have before you choose.

## COOKING EQUIPMENT

When you go camping or spend time in the woods, you need cooking equipment to make food. We suggest using a set called *Pathfinder cooking set* because it's easy to cook different types of food, clean the set, and carry it around. You can also use it as a guide to compare with other cooking sets if you want to choose a different one.

## FIRST AID

It's good to be prepared for emergencies, even if we hope they won't happen. When we're out in nature, there may not be any doctors nearby, so we need to take care of ourselves. Even a small cut can become infected and cause problems if we don't clean it properly. That's why it's important to have a first aid kit with us. At a minimum, the kit should have bandages and antiseptic wipes. But it's also a good idea to have other supplies like creams for bites and stings, gloves, and scissors. You might not need these things very often, but it's better to have them just in case.

## LIGHTING - TORCHES

When you're in the woods at night, you need a torch to see where you're going. There are two types of torches you can use: a *head torch* or a *hand-held torch*. A head torch is great because you don't have to hold it, and the light shines where you're looking. A hand-held torch is good because you can control where the light shines and change the brightness levels.

## SHELTER

When we go out in the woods, we need a safe place to stay. We can make a shelter with a special cover called a *tarp or basha*. It is strong, light, and protects us from rain and wind. If we don't have one, we can use some special blankets. We need to think about where we are going and for how long so we can plan ahead and make sure we have a good shelter.

- **Bivy**

A *bivy* is a type of shelter for sleeping outdoors that can keep you warm and protect you from insects. It's a great alternative to a tent because it's more portable and can be used in colder weather. If you haven't thought about getting one, we suggest you check it out because they're affordable and can make your outdoor experience much more enjoyable.

## PARACORD

Paracord is a really strong and tough multipurpose rope. You can use it to make a shelter, a trap, hang clothes, and much more. You can get it in different forms, like a long rope, a bracelet, or a lanyard, and in many colors. You can carry it in any way that suits you, but it's always good to have with you because it's very useful.

## SMALL KNIFE

Earlier, we talked about big knives that are useful for clearing bushes and hunting. But when it comes to smaller tasks like cutting fruits, cooked meat, or mushrooms, a small knife is much better. It's also easier to carry around because it's lighter. Just like the big knives, it's better to use a small, fixed-blade knife because they are stronger and less easy to lose. Some great examples of small bushcraft knives are the *Mora* or *Hultafor* knives.

## SHARPENER

It's very important to have a sharp knife when you're out in the woods, even if it's just for one day. You can easily sharpen your knife by using a sharpener, which you can find in many stores, or ask someone for help. If you're going to be in the woods for a while or use your knife a lot, it's best to bring the sharpener with you. That way, you'll always have a sharp knife ready when you need it!

## RUCKSACK

When you go on a trip, you need a bag to carry your things. A good bag will help you carry things easily from one place to another, but a great bag will help you carry lots of things. So, don't just pick any bag that looks cool. Take your time to choose a bag that has enough space for all your things. If you want a bag that you can use for camping and also for going to school or work, choose a smaller one with lots of straps so you can add the things you'll need for each trip. Modern bags are designed to fit your back perfectly and to keep you cool. Choose a bag that does what you need it to do and that you like.

## AXE - TOMAHAWKS - FREMONT

An axe is a big tool that can chop down small trees quickly, but it's also heavy and not good for long trips where you need to walk a lot. A *hatchet* is like a smaller, lighter version of the axe. It does a similar job, but it's easier to carry around on longer trips. However, it's not very good for doing lots of different things. Then there are *Tomahawks* and *Fremont* tools. These tools are more versatile but not as strong as an axe or hatchet. They're lightweight and great for lots of smaller tasks but not as good for bigger jobs.

## WATER CARRY

Carrying water is super important when you're out in the wild. We've already talked about how to make sure water is safe to drink, but what if there's no water around? That's when you need to bring your own!

One way to do this is by using a special bag called a *bladder*. You can get bags that are made just for bladders or backpacks that have a spot for a bladder to go in. If that's not your thing, you can also carry a water bottle on your bag or pants using a special clip.

No matter how you do it, the important thing is to have a way to carry water with you so you don't get dehydrated.

## FIRE STARTING

The last thing you need to start a fire is a special tool called a *fire starter*. There are many kinds of fire starters, so you might have to try a few to find one that works best for you. Make sure the fire starter you choose can start a fire even when it's wet outside or if you are in a high place. If you are going somewhere new, it's always a good idea to check if you have the right tools to start a fire.

## BUSHCRAFT AND NATURE: A BOND FORGED IN THE WILD

Some time ago, I went camping with my son in a big forest in Spain. When I got there, I cut down a long, straight branch from a tree so I could make my way through the bushes more easily. I was happy to find a willow tree nearby with lots of straight branches that I could use to make a strong stick for bashing. Willow trees also grow in my home country. It felt nice to see a familiar tree in a new place.

When you spend time in nature, plants and trees become more than just things that are there. You might start to feel like they are your friends because they can help you out when you need them.

It's not strange to love and respect nature. People who have lived in the wild for a long time have always had a special relationship with nature. For people who like bushcraft, spending time in nature is really helpful.

Finally, bushcraft is more than just knowing how to use tools and having the right equipment. It's also about feeling a connection with nature and respecting it. When you spend time outdoors and learn to rely on nature for what you need, you start to appreciate it more. With bushcraft, you have to work hard and use your skills to survive in the wild. You can't be lazy, or you won't make it. But it's a great way to learn about nature and feel like you're a part of it.

# NATURE'S ARCHITECTS: BUILDING SHELTERS WITH KIDS

Do you want to enjoy an active and fun time in nature? Then, building a shelter using materials you find in nature is a great way to do so. One way kids can enjoy their time in nature is to exercise their imagination and apply their problem-solving skills in nature. Parents and guardians can encourage their children to build a lovely playhouse out of natural things like sticks, vines, and stones. They can also add a path made of stones and use logs as chairs and tables. Whether it's just for one person or for the whole family, it's going to be so much fun to play in!

Learning wilderness survival skills can be a fun and exciting way to spend time with people you love. It's a great way to create lasting memories and become more confident and safer when you're in the outdoors. As you learn basic survival skills, you'll feel prepared in case of an emergency. You'll also be able to appreciate and care for the environment. It's a valuable experience that will stay with you for a lifetime.

When I was a kid, my friends and I used to build forts and shelters outside for fun. But do you know what's really important about building a shelter? It can help you stay safe in the wild and protect you from the weather. There are different types of shelters you can build, and it's important to know where to build them and how to stay safe from the sun and cold. We'll also learn about hypothermia (when your body gets too cold), and how to stay safe from it. So, if you ever find yourself outside without a proper shelter, you can remember what you will learn here and use your imagination to build one!

Let's start by learning about building shelters. We'll look first at why shelters are important in survival.

## THE IMPORTANCE OF SHELTERS IN SURVIVAL

When you're outside, having a shelter is really important for staying safe as it protects you from the weather and keeps you safe from danger, like from any animals that might be around. If it's going to rain, the shelter that can keep you dry. You can also use a tarp to cover the shelter to make it water-resistant. If it's a really hot day, you might want to make an open shelter so you can feel the breeze.

**There are Four Basic Types of Shelters that You can build:**

1. The first one is called a *lean-to shelter*. It's like a roof that leans against a tree or a rock.
2. The second type is a *debris hut*, which is made of sticks and leaves.
3. The third type is a *tarp shelter*, which uses a tarp to cover the shelter area.

4. The fourth type is an *A-frame shelter*, which looks like a tent but made of sticks and leaves.

Remember, safety is really important when you're out in the wild, so make sure to always have a shelter ready in case of emergencies.

Each shelter can be built with different materials depending on the weather at your location. Lets's take a look.

## TYPES OF NATURAL MATERIALS FOR BUILDING SHELTERS

If you want to build a shelter in nature, you can use natural materials that you find around you. Some materials you can use are:

- **Branches of different sizes:** You can use branches to make walls, roofs, and frames for your shelter. Look for branches that are strong and flexible so you can bend them without breaking.
- **Vines or twine**: Vines are plants that grow around trees or poles. You can use them to tie branches together and make your shelter stronger. If you can't find vines, you can use twine or rope instead.
- **Logs or large rocks**: Logs are big pieces of wood that you can use to make the frame of your shelter. Rocks can also be used to make walls or to hold down the edges of your shelter.
- **Small stones:** You can use small stones to make a floor for your shelter. Just make sure you pick smooth stones that won't hurt your feet.

Remember, when you use natural materials, you should always be respectful of the environment. Be kind to nature. Don't cut down living trees or damage plants. Instead, look for materials that have already fallen down from the trees, such as branches or dead wood, that you can use. You should learn about the potential risks in our area before building your shelter like watching out for things like ticks, snakes, and poison ivy that can make you sick. Have fun building your nature cubby!

## STEP-BY-STEP GUIDE TO BUILDING A SIMPLE SHELTER

Before you build the shelter, find the right location. This can be a bit tricky, but don't worry! Here are some tips:

1. **Look for a dry, flat spot.** If the ground is wet or muddy, it will make you cold at night. A flat spot will also help keep rain from running down into your shelter. You can even dig trenches to help redirect any water away from your shelter.
2. **Stay away from bodies of water.** You want to be close enough to get water easily but not too close that you get wet or washed away. Also, avoid setting up camp in valleys since cold air settles there at night.
3. **Find a spot with trees.** Trees can block the wind and help keep you warm. Look for a place with thick foliage to protect yourself from the elements and to stay hidden. If you want to be found, stay close to open areas where you can be seen.
4. **Check for any danger.** Look above the area for any signs of danger. Check for anything over your head that could cause harm to you or damage your shelter. Look for dead

tree limbs, loose rocks, or mud since these could easily break and fall down on top of you.

Remember, finding the right location for your shelter is important to keep you safe and warm.

## SHELTERS FOR SURVIVAL

- **Debris-Hut Shelter**

This type of shelter is good for keeping you warm because it uses your own body heat to keep you cozy. It has a triangular shape. The only drawback to keep in mind is that it's only big enough for two people at most. If you need more space, you can build a *lean-to shelter* instead.

Before you start building it, find a good spot to put it. Make sure the ground is flat and not bumpy and that water can drain away from your shelter so you don't get wet.

Steps to build a debris hut in a kid-friendly way:

1. Find a long piece of wood or strong stick to use as the spine of the hut. This will be the main beam of your shelter. This is the most important part because it holds everything up.
2. Put one end of the stick on a big rock or push it into the ground.
3. Find long sticks to put on top of the main beam to make the roof. You can lean them against the beam to make a triangle shape.
4. You can also bend smaller sticks over the spine to make a curved frame. This will give you enough room to lie down.
5. Start gathering lots of leaves and pile them on top the sticks to build the roof. This is the fun part! Cover the frame with lots of leaves, grass, ferns, or other natural things you can find.
6. Make sure you cover everything up tightly so that wind and rain can't get in.
7. If you have a tarp, you can put it over the leaves to keep you dry. And if you want to stay even warmer, you can fill the inside with more leaves.
8. Leave a small hole for the door and cover it partially with more debris to keep you warm.

- **Lean-To Shelter**

The Lean-To Shelter is a type of shelter that uses a tree or a solid structure as a base. You can find big branches and lean them against your base to create a roof.

This shelter is different from the *debris-hut* as it provides more space and is more stable against bad weather. But you need to build it away from the wind so that it stays strong.

To make it even more stable, dig a small trench next to your shelter. You can use a multi-tool shovel for this. This will give you more space to move around and make your shelter sturdier. Building this shelter can be a lot of fun.

Follow these simple steps to build your *lean-to shelter*:

1. Find a big and strong branch or log.
2. Lean one end of the branch against a tree or use a support to hold it up.
3. Put smaller branches or sticks against the main branch. Start from the bottom and work your way up.
4. Cover the framework with leaves, grass, or other materials to make it waterproof and keep you warm.

- **Enclosed Lean-To Shelter**

An enclosed *lean-to shelter* is a more advanced shelter than the *lean-to shelter* as it provides additional protection by covering the sides. It can protect you from harsh weather conditions and wildlife; but it's more laborious.

To build it, you'll need to use more branches to close off the sides of the shelter and tie them together with some rope to make a door. It's like building a fort in the woods.

- **Dome-Shaped Shelter**

To make a *dome-shaped shelter*, you'll need to find some long and bendy sticks called saplings.

Look for ones that are not too stiff and can be easily bent.

1. Find a flat area that's twice as wide as your arms stretched out.
2. Stick the saplings into the ground in a circle around that area. The more saplings you use, the stronger your shelter will be.
3. Tie more saplings around the circle to make the dome's shape. Make sure to use strong rope so that the saplings stay together and your shelter is stable.
4. Cover the dome with a tarp if it's raining or you want to keep the inside dry.
5. Add a roof from big leaves or branches. The more leaves you add, the warmer your shelter will be!

Build your own bed when you make any of the shelters we just mentioned. Just find two strong branches and lay down enough leaves on top to make it comfy. That way, you can have a good night's rest while camping outside!

## LEARNING FROM OUR ANCESTORS: TRADITIONAL SHELTERS AROUND THE WORLD

Next, let's look at some examples of *primitive shelters* used by our ancestors.

- **Australian Aboriginal Shelter**

Australian Aborigines were people who used to travel a lot. They hunted and gathered food as they moved within their tribal areas. Sometimes, they stopped for a few days or weeks in one place if there was enough food and water.

In the tropical north of Australia, during the wet season, people often stayed in one place for several months. They built simple shelters, known as the Australian aboriginal shelters, using bent-over stringy bark. In Australia, the weather is usually not too cold, so many people used to sleep outside under the stars to keep cool. But when the nights got chilly, they would have a small fire or two to keep them warm. Instead of having one big fire, each person would have a small fire on either side of them. They also snuggled up to their camp dogs and dingos to keep them warm, just like we use hot water bottles.

- **Gunyah-The Australian Shelter**

The *Gunyah* is a type of shelter that people used to live in long ago on the East Coast of Australia. It's made out of sticks and bark, and the bark comes from a kind of tree called Melaleuca, which is also known as "paper bark."

The Gunyah is shaped like a dome and is built using a framework of sticks. The bark is then placed on top of the sticks to create a waterproof cover. Although it's a very simple shelter, it's comfortable and keeps people dry even in the rain.

Aboriginal Australians used different types of Melaleuca trees for many things, such as building shelters, making rafts and bandages, preparing food, painting, and making blankets. They even used the nectar from the flowers to make sweet drinks. One of the most popular things that come from the Melaleuca trees today is Tea Tree Oil, which is used in many medicines like soap and ointments because it is good for fighting bacteria.

Aboriginal people didn't always move around. They sometimes lived in one place all year, or they moved to different areas depending on the season. There are stories from when the first Europeans met the Aboriginal people and saw their homes. One story, written by Robert Brough Smyth, tells us that the Aboriginal people had different types of homes. Some were under pretty yellow flowers, some were under the shade of trees, and some were made for a few people to live together. They were usually round or semi-circular with a pointy roof and a flat part that stuck out like a porch.

People in Australia built different kinds of shelters depending on where they lived and the current season. They used materials like cane, branches, grass, leaves, bark, bamboo, and even whalebone to construct their shelters. Some shelters were shaped like beehives, and others had raised platforms to protect from floods. The shelters could be simple or complex, with different spaces for various activities. People used these shelters to stay safe and comfortable in different weather conditions.

- **Wigwam**

A *wigwam* is a type of house that some Native American tribes and First Nations people used to live in. It is round and looks like a dome. Sometimes, it is called a wickiup. In some places, like the Northeastern United States, they call it a wigwam, and in the Southwestern United States, they call it a wickiup. It can be made of different materials, depending on where the people lived. The wigwam is not the same as a tipi, which is used by Native Plains people.

The *Paiute wickiup* is a type of shelter that was used by many tribes in the past. It has a round shape, which makes it perfect for use in different weather conditions. People from the Great Lakes-St. Lawrence Lowlands used to live in wigwams or longhouses.

This kind of shelter is built with arched poles made of wood that are covered with bark or other materials like grass, brush, rushes, hides, or cloth. The construction of these structures depends on the culture and the materials available in the area.

Wigwams are mostly used as seasonal shelters, although some can be more permanent. They take a longer time to build than tipis and are not as portable. In the Northeast, a typical wigwam has a curved surface that can resist tough weather conditions.

To build a wigwam, people cut down young green tree saplings of any type of wood, around 10 to 15 feet long. Then, a circle is drawn on the ground, and the saplings are bent and placed over the circle. The taller ones are used in the middle, and the shorter ones on the outside. Another set of saplings is used to wrap around the wigwam to give it support. Finally, the sides and roof are placed on it. The sides of the wigwam are usually made of bark stripped from trees, and the framing was the responsibility of the male of the family.

- **Native American Teepee**

Native American tribes, who were always on the move, needed a type of home that was easy to build and take down. They used a tent called a *Teepee*, which was made by using long wooden poles tied together to form a cone shape. They covered the frame with the hide of a buffalo or bison.

When the tribe arrived at a new place, the women and children of the tribe would quickly build the Teepees while the male were searching for the buffalo. They were so good at building them that it only took around 30 minutes!

The Teepee was a clever type of home that could be used all year round. During the summer, the hide covering could be raised up to let cool air flow in. During winter, grass was added to make it warmer. The families would build a fire in the middle of the Teepee to keep them warm.

- **Traditional African Homes**

In Africa, most people use natural materials that they find nearby to build their homes. They use grasses, hardwoods, bamboo, raffia palm, earth, and clay. In areas where there are not many natural resources, people move from place to place and live in simple brush shelters or portable tents made of animal skins and woven hair.

African houses are often round in shape. For example, the Xhosa people in southern Africa built one-room houses called *rondavels*. They make them from a circle of timber posts filled in with mud or basket weave and topped with a thatched roof. In some areas, they use sun-dried mud to construct round houses in a coil pottery technique.

However, many of the natural materials used in African architecture can easily be damaged by rain, rot, or termites. This means that even if the buildings are constructed well, they won't last for a very long time. So, many of the traditional buildings that we see today in Africa are not very old, even though they were built in styles that date back many centuries.

## ENCOURAGING RESPONSIBLE OUTDOOR PRACTICES

When you go camping, hiking, or visiting a park, it's important to be safe and respectful of the environment. Here are ten things you can do to stay safe and protect the wilderness:

- **Plan ahead:** Before you go camping or outdoors, make sure you know where you're going and what to expect. Check the weather and make sure you have everything you need.
- **Communicate**: Let someone know where you're going and when you'll be back. Bring a phone or a radio so you can call for help if you need it.
- **Bring the right gear:** Make sure you have all the gear you need for your trip. This includes things like a backpack, food and water, and a first aid kit.
- **Don't go alone:** It's always safer to go with a friend or family member. If you do go alone, make sure someone knows where you're going.
- **Practice 'leave no trace':** This means leaving the wilderness just as you found it, without leaving any trash or damaging the environment.
- **Stay in designated areas:** Stick to the trails and campsites that are marked and designated for visitors. This helps protect the environment and keeps you safe.
- **Leave wildlife alone:** As much as you might want to pet or feed the animals, it's important to let them be in the wilderness. They are wild animals and should be respected and admired from afar.
- **Hydrate:** Make sure you drink plenty of water while you're hiking or camping. It's easy to get dehydrated, especially on hot days.

- **Bring a first aid kit:** You never know when you might need it. Make sure you have one with you at all times.
- **Be mindful of your group:** If you're hiking or camping with a group, make sure everyone is comfortable and safe. Assign roles for everyone so that no one person is doing all the work.

# FINDING YOUR BEARINGS: A KID'S GUIDE TO NAVIGATING THE WILDERNESS

When we go on outdoor adventures, we may need to find your way from one place to another. This is called navigation. One way to navigate is to go in a straight line from where we are to where we want to go. But sometimes, this is not easy or safe to do. So, we use a special tool called a *compass* to help us find the right direction. We choose a direction on the compass, which is called a *bearing*, and then we walk in that direction. This helps us to stay on course and reach our destination safely.

Next, when do you take a *bearing*? Taking a bearing also means figuring out the direction you need to go in order to get to your destination. You would need to take a bearing when you want to go to a place in a straight line for example. But, the place should not be too far, and the path should be easy to walk on. If there are big rocks or trees or a swamp in the way, then it will be tough to maintain a straight line. However, there are ways to help you stay on track even when there are obstacles. It's also better to take smaller steps and check your direction again and again rather than taking a huge step and realizing later that you went the wrong way. This can happen, especially when you have to travel a long distance.

## GETTING YOUR BEARINGS: LEARNING BASIC NAVIGATION SKILLS

Knowing how to take a bearing is an important skill to learn when you're out exploring nature. It helps you in different ways, like checking which direction a path or trail is going, looking at something specific in the distance, or showing you the way to go when you're not sure. You can also use bearings to help you find your way back in case you get lost. This is called *relocation*. When you relocate, you use a bearing to point you in the direction you need to go to get back to a known location.

## SIGHTING A BEARING

If you're outside and can't see very well, you might see something important in the distance for just a moment when the clouds move. If you do, you can practice what's called *sighting a bearing*. It's like taking a picture of the direction you need to go so you don't get lost.

So, how do you *sight a bearing*? First, using a compass, follow these simple steps:

1. Hold the compass in front of you and point the direction of the travel arrow at the place you want to go to. If it's a a mountain, point it at. If it's a river, the point along the river.

2. Next, keep the compass still. Rotate the compass housing (the part with the numbers) until the red arrow is under the North arrow. You can remember this step by using a fun phrase like "red in the shed" or "mouse in the house."
3. Now, you can read the bearing along the line that's marked with numbers. This will show you the direction you need to go in order to reach your destination. Just be sure to keep the compass leveled and away from any metal objects, like zippers or phones, which can interfere with the magnetic needle in the compass.

In the pictures below, a man is *sighting a bearing* off a tall telegraph pole at a distance. He's trying to figure out which direction he needs to go, and the pole is helping him.

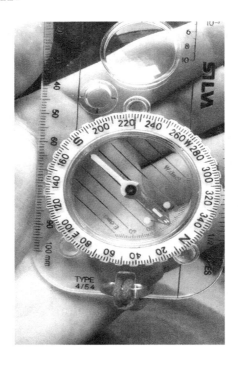

When we use a compass to find directions, we need to remember that the north magnetic needle doesn't always point exactly to the north on a map. This is called *magnetic variation*. To get an accurate direction, we need to adjust for this.

In this example, the compass shows a direction of 226 degrees. Let's say the magnetic variation is 1 degree. To transfer this direction to a map, we need to subtract 1 degree from 226 to make it 225 degrees. This way, we can be sure we're heading in the right direction!

## TAKING A GRID BEARING

When we go hiking or camping, we use a map to guide us. Sometimes, we need to check which direction we should go in. To do this, we take a *grid bearing* from the map. It helps us to know which way we should walk. We can also take more bearings while we walk to make sure we're still going in the right direction. It's like using a compass to find our way, but using a map instead.

To take a *grid bearing*, follow these steps:

1. Estimate the bearing from your current position to your next checkpoint. For example, if you're heading northeast, you should expect a bearing between 0 and 90 degrees.
2. Use a line on the compass to link your position on the map to your next checkpoint. Make sure that the direction of the travel arrow on the compass is pointing toward your next checkpoint on the map.
3. Next, keep the compass fixed on the map and rotate the compass housing so that the orienting arrows are parallel to the North-South lines on the map. Make sure that the orienting arrow is pointing towards the grid north. Once you have done this, remove the compass from the map and hold it flat in front of you with the direction of the travel arrow facing away from you.
4. Now, rotate your body until both the orienting arrow and the north magnetic arrow align. This is similar to *sighting a bearing*. Once the arrows are aligned, the direction of the travel arrow will be pointing in the direction you need to travel. You can now use this bearing to navigate to your next checkpoint.
5. You can read the bearing from the index line. But take note of this so you don't forget or move the compass housing by mistake.

## CHECKING THE DIRECTION OF HANDRAILS

There are two ways to use a compass to check which direction to go: *sighting* and *grid bearing*. Both of these methods can help us stay safe and avoid getting lost.

*Sighting* is when we look at a feature on the ground, like a path or a tree, and then look at the same feature on our map. We can then use our compass to draw a line between where we are and where we want to go. This helps us stay on the right path.

*Grid bearing* is when we use our map to plan our route in advance. We can then use our compass to measure the angle between our current location and the path we want to take. We can then follow the path that matches the angle we measured on our compass.

When using a compass to figure out where you are, make sure you don't hold it too close to things that have metal in them, like zippers, phones, or water bottles. Also, be careful around magnetic clips and walking poles.

There's a saying that helps you remember how to use the compass: "Grid to Mag ADD, Mag to Grid, GET RID." This means that when you're going from the map to the compass, you add the magnetic variation.

When you're going from the compass to the map, you subtract it. And when you're done, you should put your compass away so it doesn't mess up your directions. Just remember that this saying might not be accurate in a few years because magnetic north is moving east of grid north.

## TOOLS OF THE TRADE: MAP READING AND COMPASS USE

A *compass* is like a magic tool that can help you find your way when you're out exploring nature. It's like a map, but better! If you learn how to use it, you'll never get lost. All you need to do is figure out which way is north, and the compass will tell you which way to go. It's so easy, and with a little practice, you'll be a pro at navigating in no time! Let's look at some of the steps to using a compass.

### COMPACT BASICS

- **Understand the Layout of the Compass**

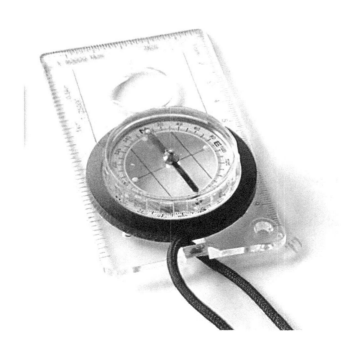

To use a compass, you need to understand its basic parts. Here are the components of a compass that you should get to know:

1. **Baseplate:** This is a clear, plastic plate that holds the compass.
2. **The direction of travel arrow:** This arrow points away from the compass and shows you the direction you want to go.
3. **Compass housing:** The compass housing is a clear, plastic circle that has a magnetized needle inside.
4. **Degree dial:** The degree dial is a twistable dial that surrounds the compass housing and shows all 360 degrees of the circle.
5. **Magnetic needle:** This is the needle that spins inside the compass housing and points towards the Earth's magnetic field.
6. **Orienting arrow:** The orienting arrow is a non-magnetic arrow inside the compass housing that helps you align the compass with a map.
7. **Orienting lines:** These are the lines inside the compass housing that run parallel to the orienting arrow. They also help you align the compass with a map.

So, if you want to use a compass, you need to understand these parts and how they work together.

- **Hold the Compass Correctly**

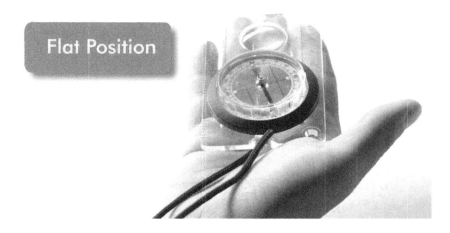

Hold the compass flat in your hand and your hand close to your chest. That's the right way to use it when you're walking or hiking. If you're also using a map, make sure the map is flat on a surface, and then place the compass on top of the map. This will help you get a more accurate reading.

- **Find Out Where You're Facing**

Follow these steps to find out with your compass which direction you are facing:

1. Look at the magnetic needle of the compass.
2. Turn the degree dial on the compass until the orienting arrow lines up with the magnetic arrow, pointing them both North.
3. Look at the direction of the travel arrow on the compass to find the general direction you are facing. If the arrow is between the N and the E, you are facing Northeast. If it is between the N and the W, you are facing Northwest. And so on.

4. Find the intersection point of the direction of the travel arrow and the degree dial on the compass. Look closely at the degree markers to take a more accurate reading. If it intersects at 23, for example, you are facing 23 degrees Northeast.

Remember to hold the compass level and away from any metal objects, as they can interfere with the magnetic needle.

- **Understand the Difference Between "True" North and "Magnetic" North**

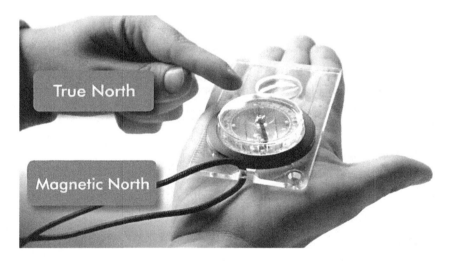

When you use the compass, it's important to understand the difference between "true" North and "magnetic" North. Here are some basic things to keep in mind:

1. True North or Map North is the point at which all longitudinal lines meet on a map, at the North Pole. It's at the top of the map, and all maps are laid out the same way.

2. Remember that the compass won't point to True North because of slight variations in the magnetic field. Instead, it'll point to Magnetic North.
3. Magnetic North refers to the tilt of the magnetic field, which is about eleven degrees from the tilt of the Earth's axis. This means that the difference between True North and Magnetic North can be as many as 20 degrees in some places.
4. Depending on where you are on the Earth, you'll need to account for this magnetic shift to get an accurate reading with your compass.
5. Even though the difference between True North and Magnetic North may seem small, it can add up over distance. For example, if you travel just one degree off for the distance of a mile, you'll end up about 100 feet (30.5 m) off course. That means you'll be even more off track after ten or twenty miles! To compensate for this, you need to take the declination (the difference between True North and Magnetic North) into account when you use your compass.

- **Learn to Correct for Declination**

Finding North in your compass may not be the same as the North on your map. This is because of *declination*, which is the difference between True North and Magnetic North. Correcting for declination will make it easier to use the compass. The correction will be different depending on your location.

1. In the US, there's the *zero declination line* that goes through Alabama, Illinois, and Wisconsin. The declination is zero when the two poles align.

2. East of this line, you have to subtract some degrees from your compass reading, and West of it, you'll need to add some degrees.
3. You can find out the declination in your area and adjust your compass reading accordingly.

## USING THE COMPASS

- **Gather Your Bearings to Find Out Which Direction You're Headed.**

To ensure you're heading in the right direction when hiking or camping in the woods or fields, it's important to periodically check your bearings. Here are the steps to do so:

1. Hold the compass flat in your hand and make sure the direction of the travel arrow is pointing in the direction you've been traveling and intend to continue traveling.
2. Unless you're heading north, the magnetic needle will spin off to one side.
3. Twist the degree dial until the orienting arrow lines up with the north end of the magnetic needle. This will tell you the direction of your travel arrow.
4. Check the degree dial for the local magnetic variation and twist it the correct number of degrees to the left or right depending on the declination.
5. See where the direction of the travel arrow lines up with the degree dial to know your exact direction.

By following these simple steps, you can avoid getting lost and stay on track while enjoying your outdoor activities.

- **Don't Stop Moving in this Direction**

To find your way with the compass, first make sure you hold it the right way. Then, turn your body until the needle on the compass points to the top of the map. Follow the arrow on the compass to go in the right direction. Remember to check the compass often, but be careful not to move the dial by mistake.

- **Stay Focused on Points in The Distance**

Focus on points in the distance to stay on track. To do this, first, look down at the direction of the travel arrow on your compass. Then, find a distant object, like a tree or telephone pole, and use it as a guide to walk in the right direction. Be sure to choose an object that's not too far away, as big objects like mountains aren't accurate enough to navigate by.

If you can't see any distant objects due to limited visibility, you can use a member of your walking party to help guide you. Stand still and ask them to walk in the direction indicated by the arrow on your compass. As they walk, call out to them to correct their direction if needed. Once they reach the edge of your visibility, ask them to wait for you to catch up. Repeat this process as many times as needed to stay on track.

- **Change the Direction of Travel on Your Map**

Place your map on a flat surface and put the compass on top of it. Make sure the arrow on the compass is pointing to the top of the map, which is true north. If you know where you are on the map, move the compass around until the edge of it lines up with your location, and the arrow still points north.

Next, draw a line on the map along the edge of the compass that goes through your location. If you walk along this line, you will be going in the right direction to get to where you want to go. Just remember to keep following the line you drew on the map to stay on course.

- **Learn to Take a Bearing from the Map**

Place the map on a flat (horizontal) surface and put the compass on the map. Then, line up the compass so that it points from where you are to where you want to go. You can use the edge of the compass to draw a line on the map to show the way.

Next, turn the compass dial until the little arrow on it is pointing to the top of the map, which is called "true north." This will help you know which way is north, south, east, and west. Make sure the compass lines up with the map's lines. Once you've done this, you can put the map away.

Fields are not perfectly symmetrical. The complexity of the geomagnetic field is demonstrated through *declination* (also called *magnetic variation*), so you need to account for declination and make the necessary adjustments to your compass to make sure you're going the right way. Declination will be positive when the angle is east of true north (also known as *East declination*), and will be negative when its angle is west (also known as *West declination*).

In places with *West declination*, you'll need to add some degrees to your compass reading, while in places with *East declination*, you'll need to subtract some degrees. Remember, this is different from when you first took your bearing, so it's important to pay attention to these changes.

- **Navigate with the New Bearings**

Hold the compass flat and make sure the arrow pointing where you want to go is in front of you. Move your body until the needle inside the compass points to the top of the compass. When it's pointing the right way, you can start walking, and it will guide you to your destination.

- **If You Get Lost: Remain Calm, Cool, and Collected**

If you get lost, you don't need to panic. Just stay calm, collected, and relaxed. Don't get anxious. Use the instructions below to help you find your way back.

1. **Pick out three well-known sites that you can see and find them on the map.** When you're lost, it's important to figure out where you are on a map. One way to do this is by finding three big landmarks that you can both see and locate on the map. It can be hard, but it's very helpful! Look around you and find things like big buildings, mountains, or lakes that you can see in different directions. Once you've found three, you can use them to figure out where you are on the map.
2. **Point your directional arrow towards the first landmark.** After you've found a landmark, point the arrow on the compass toward it. The compass will show you which direction you should go in. If you are not facing north, you will need to turn the compass until the arrow lines up with the north end of the needle. This will show you which way is north. Finally, depending on where you are, you may need to adjust the compass to make sure it is pointing in the right direction.

3. **Change the direction of the landmark on your map.** If you get lost you can change the direction of the landmark on your map by following these steps. Again, find a landmark like a big building or a mountain that you can see in real life and on your map. Then, put your map on a table or a flat surface and place your compass on the map. Turn the compass until the direction arrow is pointing to the north on the map. Now, move the compass until the edge of the compass goes through the landmark on the map.

4. **Triangulate your position.** To triangulate, you need to draw three lines on your map. To draw them, use the compass and find three landmarks that you can see. Start drawing the first line by following the compass and going through your approximate position. Now, repeat the process for the other two landmarks. Once you have drawn all three lines, you will have a triangle on your map. Your position is somewhere inside this triangle. If your lines are really accurate, they will meet at one point, and you will know exactly where you are.

## TRAILBLAZING 101: LEAVING MARKS TO FIND YOUR WAY BACK

Remember that it's important to be prepared in case you get lost. So, in addition to the above, if you do get lost, there are other things you can do to help you find the way back.

First, don't panic. Take a deep breath and try to stay calm. Then, look around for things you recognize, like mountains, rivers, or roads. If you have a map or compass, use it to help you figure out where you are.

If you can't find any landmarks, try to follow a stream or river downstream. This can lead you to civilization, where you can find help.

If you're still lost, climb to a higher point, like a hill or a tree. This will give you a better view of the area and help you spot landmarks or signs of civilization.

You can also use the sun or stars to help you figure out which direction to go. If you have a compass, use it along with the sun or stars to help you navigate.

If you're really stuck and need help, make noise by yelling, whistling, or using a device that can be heard at a distance. Also, leave signs like rocks, branches, or anything else you can find to create a trail or mark your path.

But the best way to avoid getting lost is to be prepared. Bring a GPS (Global Positioning System). The GPS helps to provide you with positioning, navigation, and timing services (PTN). Also bring a map, carry a whistle and communication devices, and tell people where you're going and when you plan to come back. This way, if you do get lost, people will know where to look for you.

# CONCRETE JUNGLE: MASTERING URBAN SURVIVAL SKILLS

*I*magine a world where skyscrapers replace the trees—a world where the rivers are made of asphalt. Yes, you've guessed it - we're discussing the Concrete Jungle! This chapter will dive into the exciting world of **urban survival skills**, where the city becomes our playground. We must speak of the urban cities as much as we talk about the bush because we can apply our urban survival skills when we get to the bush. Also, we must understand that survival skills are not limited to the jungle.

Let's rewind a bit. Remember when you went for a walk with your family, and suddenly, the city seemed like a giant puzzle waiting to be solved? That's precisely what our adventure is all about. It's like being a detective in a world of towering mysteries and bustling excitement.

Now, close your eyes and imagine standing at the edge of a busy street. Cars zoom by, people hustle and bustle, and you're there, thinking of how to maneuver through the maze that's the city. Regardless of how daunting the task might seem, you can tackle it easily, which we'll explore in this chapter. Therefore, let's quickly examine some of these necessary survival skills.

## SURVIVAL SKILL NUMBER ONE

**The Art of Observation:** Like a superhero with a keen eye, you'll learn to notice small details that others might miss. It could be a quirky alley with colorful graffiti or a hidden garden amidst the skyscrapers. It's like discovering hidden treasures right in the middle of the city!

## SURVIVAL SKILL NUMBER TWO

**Navigating the Concrete Maze:** Have you ever felt like a tiny ant surrounded by tall buildings? Fear not! We'll unravel the mysteries of maps, street signs, and landmarks that will turn you into a city explorer extraordinaire.

## SURVIVAL SKILL NUMBER THREE

**Conquering the Weather:** When skies turn grey, and rain starts to fall in the city, we need this third survival skill. From mastering the art of umbrella handling to finding shelter in unexpected places, you'll be the raindrop-dodging champion of the urban jungle.

As our adventure unfolds, you'll soon discover that the city is not just a place of hustle and bustle; it's a playground filled with challenges and surprises. So, gear up, intrepid urban bushcrafters! This chapter is dedicated to helping you master the art of survival in the Concrete Jungle. Get ready to unlock the secrets of the cityscape and embark on an adventure like no other.

## NAVIGATING THE CONCRETE MAZE

One aspect of conquering your fear of the cityscape is navigating the maze. Finding your way in the city is as crucial as mastering wilderness navigation. So, let's dive into the fascinating world of city navigation, where streets turn canyons and skyscrapers become your landmarks!

## UNDERSTANDING THE CITY LAYOUT

Just like you learned to read the signs of the bush, decoding the city's layout is your first step to becoming a city navigation expert. Many U.S. cities, for instance, have a grid system, like giant checkerboards, with streets running north to south and east to west. Understanding this grid makes it easier to figure out where you are and where you want to go.

In the city, buildings aren't just structures; they're like friendly giants guiding your way. Schools, parks, and unique buildings become your urban beacons. If you can spot the school with the bright red door or the park with the giant statue, you're well on your way to becoming a city navigator.

Now, let's talk about a superhero tool for city navigation – public transport maps! Buses and subways crisscross the city; their maps are like treasure maps leading you to your destination. Learn to read the symbols and colors on these maps; they're your secret codes to unlock the city's mysteries.

Subway and bus maps are like magical scrolls filled with symbols and colors. Each line and station have its unique mark. Take the time to decipher these symbols; soon, you'll be navigating the city like a wizard casting spells. Advocacy groups like the American

Public Transportation Association even have cool resources to help you master the art of public transport.

## TECH TOOLS: YOUR URBAN SIDEKICK

In the city, we have modern magic wands – technology! Google Maps and similar services are like wizards showing you the way. However, although these tools are powerful, they often require the internet and depend on your device's battery. So, use them wisely, and don't forget to develop your navigation superpowers.

Imagine you're a superhero with a high-tech gadget and an ancient, magical compass. That's you in the city! Tech tools are fantastic, but don't forget your inner compass – the power of your senses. Look around, smell the city air, and listen to the sounds. Your senses are like secret weapons guiding you through the urban maze.

- **Quick Exercise**

Let's turn city navigation into a quest! Imagine you're on a treasure hunt, and the treasure is reaching your destination. Challenge yourself to find three landmarks on your way to school or identify five subway stations. The city is your playground, and every corner holds a new mystery to solve.

As you become a city navigation expert, you're earning your very own badge of honor. Create a neighborhood map, mark your favorite landmarks, and show it to your friends. You're not just finding your way but becoming a city explorer, and the concrete jungle is your playground.

In the world of city navigation, you're not just a traveler but an explorer armed with knowledge and curiosity. Remember the grid system, follow your urban beacons, decipher the magical transport maps, and use tech tools wisely. As you navigate the concrete maze, you're not just finding your way – you're conquering the city!

Now that you're adequately equipped, gear up, put on your explorer hat, and let the urban adventure begin. The city awaits your discoveries, and with every step, you're not just walking; you're navigating, exploring, and claiming your place in the thrilling concrete jungle. Happy navigating, brave adventurers!

## URBAN SHELTERS - FINDING SAFE HAVENS IN THE CITY

Having conquered the intricacies of city navigation, it's time to delve into another critical skill – the art of finding safe havens in the urban landscape. We'll explore the importance of identifying secure public spaces, recognizing safety signs, and mastering the urban safety basics. Get ready to unlock the secrets of urban shelters, where buildings become allies, and knowledge becomes your shield.

## SAFE HAVENS: ISLANDS OF SECURITY IN THE CITY

In the city, shelter takes on a different form. It's not about cozy nests or hidden dens; it's about finding safe, public, and populated places that offer refuge and assistance. Imagine libraries, community centers, or police stations as your urban sanctuaries – places where you can seek help, find solace, and regroup in times of need. These structures are not just buildings but your allies in the urban wilderness.

Just as you need to learn to identify edible plants in the bush, You must also learn to recognize safe places in the city. One of the urban explorer's secret tools is the ability to spot distinctive signs indicating safety. Keep an eye out for symbols like "Safe Place," which is part of a national youth outreach program in the U. S. When you see these signs, you know you've found a place ready to assist and provide a safe haven.

When walking around the city, stick to well-lit populated areas as if they were the guiding constellations in your urban sky. These areas are your protective shield against the unknown. Conversely, avoid shadowy or deserted locations, treating them like hidden traps in your urban quest. Your safety is enhanced when you stay within the well-lit realms where community and assistance thrive. Stay away from dark alleys or vacant buildings. In the urban landscape, these are akin to hidden dungeons, and we want to keep you in the well-lit realms where safety reigns supreme. Trust your instincts and avoid areas that feel unsafe.

## BUDDY SYSTEM: THE POWER OF URBAN COMPANIONSHIP

Even superheroes have sidekick. In the city, your family and friends are your trusty allies. Stick together when navigating the urban jungle. There's strength in numbers, and having a buddy adds an extra layer of protection. It's like having a shield in your urban adventure, where each team member watches out for the others.

Before embarking on any quest, brave explorers practice their moves. Create safety drills with your family. Pretend scenarios where you identify safe places, stay in well-lit areas, and avoid shadowy dangers. The more you practice, the more confident and prepared you'll be in your urban adventures. Think of it as your urban superhero training, where you hone your skills for any challenge.

Knowledge is your shield in the city, and awareness is your sword. Stay informed about your surroundings. Know where the safe havens are, recognize the signs, and be aware of your environment. Your urban shield and sword will keep you ready for any challenge that comes your way. Develop the ability to read the city's signals, understand the safety language, and be proactive in creating your safe path through the urban landscape.

Remember that you're not just a city navigator but a wise and prepared explorer. Urban shelters are your havens, your sanctuaries amid the bustling cityscape. So, keep your eyes open, stay in the light, and trust your instincts. The city is full of wonders, but armed with your newfound knowledge, you'll navigate its streets with confidence and wisdom. Happy exploring, brave city adventurers! May your urban sanctuary always be within reach, offering comfort and security amid the vibrant city tapestry.

## URBAN FORAGING - DISCOVERING UNSEEN RESOURCES IN THE CITY

Now that we've honed our city navigation skills and learned to find safe havens, it's time to move to another part of our urban adventure – the art of urban foraging. While we may not be hunting for wild berries, we're on a quest to identify the city's hidden resources. Our treasures include water fountains, public restrooms, cafes, and even edible plants in city parks.

In the city, foraging takes a different form. It's not about tracking elusive animals or spotting wild berries; it's about identifying resources tucked away in the urban labyrinth. Let's begin with one of the most crucial resources – water. Water fountains, public restrooms, and cafes can be unexpected oases in the city, offering hydration when needed.

## FOOD AND WATER: ESSENTIALS FOR YOUR EXPLORATION

Imagine your water bottle as a trusty sidekick in your urban quest. As you explore the cityscape, always carry a water bottle and refill it whenever you come across a clean water source. Staying hydrated is not just a quest requirement; it's a superhero move to keep you energized and ready for any challenge.

Now, let's embark on a food quest in the city. While you won't be hunting wild game, edible resources await discovery. Consider city parks as your foraging grounds. The Urban Foraging Guide from the Seattle Department of Parks and Recreation is your treasure map, revealing the edible plants that dot the city landscape.

City parks are like nature's grocery stores, offering a variety of edible plants. From berries to greens, these urban landscapes provide an opportunity to connect with the natural world even amidst the concrete jungle. Take time to explore, identify, and appreciate the edible treasures that city parks hold.

Just as every adventurer has a code, urban foragers have guidelines, too. The golden rule is to ask for permission before foraging in public spaces. Respect the environment and ensure that the plants you encounter are safe to eat. The city might be our playground, but it's essential to tread lightly and responsibly.

As you embark on your urban foraging adventure, look beyond the concrete jungle. Discover the beauty in unexpected places – a wild herb thriving near a sidewalk or a cluster of berries in a city square. These unseen treasures are reminders that nature coexists with the urban landscape, offering its gifts to those who take the time to observe and appreciate.

Once you've identified edible plants, it's time to unleash your culinary creativity. Imagine turning city park finds into delicious treats – a salad with foraged greens or a berry-infused dessert. The city becomes your kitchen, and every foraged ingredient is a flavored addition to your culinary creations.

## COMMUNITY CONNECTION: SHARING THE FORAGING SPIRIT

As you explore the hidden resources of the city, consider sharing your foraging spirit with the community. Organize a foraging expedition with friends or family. Share your knowledge about edible plants and the art of responsible foraging. Building a community that appreciates and respects the urban environment creates a positive ripple effect for people and the cityscape.

In concluding our foraging adventure in the cityscape, remember that urban exploration is not just about finding your way or seeking shelter; it's about discovering the richness within the bustling streets and parks. Water fountains, edible plants, and unexpected treasures are woven into the city's fabric, waiting to be explored.

So, carry your water bottle, don your explorer hat, and venture into the city with a keen eye for the unseen resources that abound. The city is not just a concrete jungle; it's a dynamic ecosystem with gifts for those who approach it with curiosity and respect. Happy foraging!

## EMERGENCY CONTACTS - THE IMPORTANCE OF CONNECTION

As we continue our journey through urban survival skills, we now focus on a critical aspect of preparedness – understanding the importance of emergency contacts. In the city, where every alley has a story, knowing whom to reach out to in times of need is your beacon of safety. Let's explore the significance of memorizing essential phone numbers, understanding when to dial 911, and utilizing modern tools like emergency alert systems.

## THE POWER OF MEMORIZATION: ESSENTIAL PHONE NUMBERS

In the world of urban exploration, knowledge is your greatest ally. Begin your training by memorizing essential phone numbers. These are the magical keys that unlock the doors to help and support. Think of your parents' work and cell numbers as your first set of keys – vital connections that bridge the gap between you and your guardians. Include trusted neighbors in your list, creating a network of support within your community. And don't forget the non-emergency number for local law enforcement; it's your hotline for assistance when urgency is not paramount.

Now, let's talk about a universal code that every city explorer should know – 911. This three-digit combination is your direct line to emergency services. When faced with a situation that requires immediate attention, dial 911. Whether it's a medical emergency, a fire, or any situation where urgent assistance is needed, 911 is your lifeline. Remember to stay calm, provide clear information, and follow the instructions given by the emergency operator.

To understand the significance of 911, let's turn to the National Emergency Number Association (NENA). This organization provides valuable resources and tips to educate kids about the importance of 911. Explore their materials, engage in interactive learning, and empower yourself with the knowledge to be a capable and confident caller during emergencies. Learning about 911 is not just a skill; it's a superpower that every young city explorer should possess.

## MODERN TOOLS FOR MODERN HEROES: EMERGENCY ALERT SYSTEMS

In today's world, technology is a powerful ally in times of crisis. Explore the capabilities of emergency alert systems on your devices. In the U.S., the Wireless Emergency Alerts (WEA) system sends critical information during emergencies. These alerts, like digital messages from a superhero headquarters, keep you informed and prepared for potential dangers in your vicinity. Familiarize yourself with enabling and receiving these alerts on your devices, turning your gadgets into essential tools for urban survival.

## THE ABCS OF EMERGENCY ALERTS: A GUIDE FOR YOUNG HEROES

Understanding emergency alert systems is like decoding a secret language. The ABCs will guide you:

- **A: Activate Alerts** - Ensure emergency alerts are activated on your devices. Check your settings to enable notifications from WEA or similar systems.
- **B: Be Informed** - Stay informed about the types of alerts and what they signify. Whether it's severe weather, Amber Alerts, or other critical information, being aware empowers you to respond effectively.
- **C: Communicate** - Share your knowledge with friends and family. Teach them about the importance of emergency alerts and how to stay connected during crises.

As a city explorer, think of your emergency contacts and alert systems as a network of interconnected dots. Each dot represents a vital link to safety and support. Your memorized phone numbers, understanding of 911, and utilization of emergency alert systems weave a safety net that envelops you in times of need.

Always remember that preparedness is like a thread weaving through the fabric of your urban adventures. Memorizing essential phone numbers, understanding 911, and embracing modern tools like emergency alert systems make you a city explorer and a vigilant guardian of your safety.

So, young adventurer, commit those essential numbers to memory, understand the power of 911, and embrace the technological tools that make you a modern urban champion. Your preparedness is the thread that binds you to safety, ensuring that you navigate the cityscape with confidence and resilience. Stay connected, stay informed, and continue your journey as the vigilant guardian of the urban realm.

## URBAN SAFETY PRECAUTIONS - STAYING SAFE IN THE CITY

As we dig deeper into the cityscape, let's unravel the secrets of staying safe in the city. Urban exploration is an exhilarating quest, but wisdom and awareness are your greatest allies. Therefore, we'll discuss the importance of staying vigilant, navigating without distractions, understanding "stranger danger," and establishing safety measures that ensure you are the master of your urban adventures.

- **Staying Aware of Surroundings**

Picture yourself as a guardian of the city, with a watchful eye on everything around you. Staying aware of your surroundings is your superpower. Keep your senses sharp, and avoid wearing headphones or keeping the volume low when walking. The sounds of the city are your clues – from the hum of traffic to the rustle of leaves, each sound tells a story.

In the city, distractions can be like invisible shadows, pulling your attention away from the present. Whether you're walking to school or exploring a park, keep your ears wide open. This doesn't mean avoiding music altogether but finding a balance that allows you to enjoy your tunes while staying attuned to the urban symphony around you.

- **Navigating the Social Landscape**

Urban exploration involves not just the physical landscape but the social one, too. Let's talk about "stranger danger" – the phrase that empowers you to navigate the social landscape wisely. If approached by someone you don't know, maintain a safe distance and be ready to seek help. The National Crime Prevention Council provides valuable resources to teach kids about recognizing and responding to stranger danger.

Imagine your journey through the city as a quest with checkpoints. Always inform a trusted adult about where you're going. Let someone know your destination, whether it's a friend's house, the park, or a local library. This simple step ensures that a guardian watches over your urban adventure, ready to assist if needed.

Also, every explorer has a map; yours is a set of agreed routes and times. Whether walking to school, biking to a friend's house, or exploring the city's wonders, stick to the routes and times agreed upon with your guardians. This ensures your safety and creates a sense of predictability in your urban quest.

In emergencies, a family safe word is your beacon of communication. Discuss and establish a safe word with your family. This word becomes a signal that something is amiss, prompting immediate action. It's a superhero call for assistance, ensuring you and your guardians are in sync even when faced with unexpected challenges.

## THE CITY'S CODE OF SAFETY: A RECAP

In navigating the city with wisdom, remember the code:

- **Guardian's Watch:** Stay aware of your surroundings.
- **Ears Wide Open:** Navigate without distractions.
- **Stranger Danger 101:** Understand and respond to the social landscape.
- **Trusted Paths:** Always inform a trusted adult about your whereabouts.
- **Sticking to the Map:** Follow agreed routes and times.
- **Family Safe Word:** Establish a beacon for emergencies.

As we conclude our exploration of urban safety precautions, remember you are more than just a city explorer. You are a wise and vigilant guardian of your safety. The city is your vast playground, and with wisdom and awareness, you navigate its streets with confidence and resilience.

So, keep your senses sharp, stay connected with trusted adults, and let the city unfold its wonders before you. Your safety is not just a precaution but a declaration of mastery over the urban landscape. Happy navigating, brave adventurer! May your quests be filled with wisdom, awareness, and the thrill of urban discovery.

# NATURE'S BOUNTY - SAFE AND SAVVY FORAGING FOR YOUNG EXPLORERS

*A*s we step into the next chapter of our exploration guide, we're about to embark on a thrilling journey into the heart of nature's bounty. Get ready to unlock the secrets of safe and savvy foraging, where every leaf, flower, and hidden treasure becomes a story waiting to be discovered. This chapter will delve into the art of understanding foraging beyond finding food. It's about connecting with the natural world, recognizing green treasures, and embracing the tiny wonders of the bush for curious explorers like you.

Nature's bounty is not just about survival; it's a call to adventure echoing through the rustling leaves and the babbling brooks. As young explorers, you are about to witness the magic of foraging, where the landscape transforms into a canvas of flavors and textures waiting to be explored. The bush, your enchanting playground, holds mysteries beyond the ordinary, inviting you to become observers and active participants in its intricate dance.

In this chapter, we will unfold the layers of *foraging*, revealing that it's more than just finding food. It's about understanding the language of the land, identifying edible plants, and embracing the tiny protein powerhouses that insects offer. Nature's bounty is a rich tapestry; you are the storytellers, uncovering the tales written in every leaf, petal, and buzzing insect.

Imagine a world where every green leaf is a treasure waiting to be discovered. We'll guide you through recognizing edible plants, understanding their flavors, and appreciating their role in the ecosystem. The bush is not just a source of sustenance; it's a verdant landscape offering a palette of tastes and textures for the adventurous palate.

As you venture deeper into nature's bounty, prepare to meet the tiny protein powerhouses – insects. From crunchy crickets to zesty ants, these miniature marvels offer a world of culinary possibilities. Foraging for insects is not just a survival skill; it's an exploration of sustainable practices and a journey into the rich tapestry of biodiversity that surrounds you.

Foraging is not merely a means of survival; it's a gateway to a culinary adventure like no other. Picture yourself experimenting with recipes, incorporating foraged ingredients into your meals, and discovering the gastronomic delights hidden within the bush. In this chapter, you become both the explorer and the chef, creating a unique blend of flavors that profoundly connect you to the land.

Nature's bounty is a treasure trove of experiences waiting to be embraced. Beyond the ordinary lies a journey into curiosity and connection. Every foraged discovery becomes a thread woven into the fabric of your exploration, connecting you to the bush in ways that go beyond the surface. As you navigate the intricate world of foraging, may your curiosity be your guide, and may every leaf and insect tell a story that becomes a part of your own.

As we embark on this chapter of Nature's Bounty, envision yourself stepping into a world where the bush is not just a landscape but a canvas of green treasures and tiny wonders. With each foraged discovery, you're not just exploring; you're becoming a part of a story that unfolds with every step. So, young explorers, fasten your explorer's hat, open your senses to the symphony of the bush, and let the journey into nature's bounty begin!

## UNDERSTANDING FORAGING - MORE THAN JUST FINDING FOOD

Welcome, young explorers, to the heart of the bush. The art of foraging is a cluster of curiosity, connection, and the thrill of discovery. In this chapter, we dive deep into the essence of foraging, exploring the notion that it's more than just finding food. It's an immersive journey that transcends the basic survival instinct, inviting you to understand the bush as a living, breathing ecosystem where every leaf, flower, and insect has a role to play.

Before we delve into the intricacies of foraging, let's take a moment to appreciate the symphony of the bush. Picture it as a vibrant orchestra, each element contributing to the harmony of the whole. The rustle of leaves, the buzz of insects, and the melodious calls of birds play their part in this grand composition. Understanding foraging is akin to learning the notes of this symphony, where you become not just an audience but an active participant.

## FORAGING BEYOND HUNGER

Traditionally, foraging has been associated with the primal need for sustenance. However, our journey today transcends the basic instinct of hunger. It's about adopting a holistic approach that embraces the ecological, cultural, and spiritual dimensions of foraging. The bush becomes a classroom, and you, the eager student, learn to read its lessons written in the patterns of leaves, the colors of flowers, and the rhythms of life.

To understand foraging, one must learn the language of the land. The bush communicates through subtle signals – the growth patterns of plants, the timing of blossoms, and the interactions between species. As you navigate this living ecosystem, you begin to decipher the messages it conveys. A budding flower may signal the onset of a particular season. At the same time, the presence of certain plants could indicate the ecosystem's health. Foraging becomes a conversation with nature where you learn to listen as much as you learn to seek.

For many communities worldwide, foraging is not just a survival skill; it's a cultural legacy passed down through generations. Elders become storytellers, sharing the wisdom embedded in the act of foraging. Every plant and insect have a tale; through foraging, you become a bearer of these cultural narratives. It's an intergenerational conversation where the land becomes a living archive of stories to be explored.

The act of foraging transcends the physical and enters the realm of the spiritual. It's about nurturing a connection with the land beyond the tangible. As you pluck a leaf or observe a butterfly, there's a sense of communion with something greater than yourself. Foraging becomes a spiritual practice to center oneself amid the natural world's vastness.

Understanding foraging also involves embracing a set of ethics that respect the delicate balance of ecosystems. It's not a free-for-all gathering; it's a mindful exploration where you take only what you need and leave the rest undisturbed. The ethics of foraging teach you to be a responsible steward of the land, ensuring that your quest contributes to the thriving biodiversity rather than disrupting it.

In the bush, timing is everything. The seasonal dance dictates when certain plants bloom, fruits ripen, and insects emerge. Understanding the temporal rhythms of the bush enhances your foraging skills. It's not just about finding food; it's about synchronizing with the natural calendar, becoming attuned to the cyclical patterns that govern life in the wilderness.

Foraging is not limited to plants alone; it extends to the tiny wonders that often go unnoticed. Insects, often overlooked, are integral to the ecosystem. As you explore foraging beyond food, you discover insects' role in pollination, soil health, and even pest control. They become your allies in the intricate dance of the bush, offering lessons in interconnectedness and symbiosis.

## EDUCATIONAL EXCURSION: FORAGING AS A LEARNING ADVENTURE

Consider foraging as an educational excursion, a learning adventure where each step unveils a new discovery. Identify plants using guidebooks or smartphone apps, observe insect behavior, and note the changes in the landscape with each season. Foraging becomes a holistic educational experience that integrates science, ecology, and cultural studies, transforming the bush into an open-air classroom.

As we conclude this exploration into understanding foraging, envision it as a tapestry woven with threads of knowledge, respect, and appreciation. It's more than just finding food; it's a journey that encompasses ecology, culture, and spirituality. So, young explorer, step into the bush with open eyes and heart. The language of the land awaits your interpretation, and the lessons it imparts will shape not just your foraging skills but your understanding of the interconnected web of life. Happy foraging, brave adventurer! May the bush reveal its secrets to you, one leaf at a time.

## RECOGNIZING EDIBLE PLANTS - GREEN TREASURES

Building your green library of knowledge is one of the first steps in recognizing edible plants. Books like the "National Audubon Society Field Guide to North American Plants" are invaluable companions in this exploration. These guides provide detailed descriptions, vivid illustrations, and key characteristics in plant identification. Imagine your book as a treasure map, guiding you to the riches of the bush. Flip through its pages, study the images, and let the adventure begin.

For our young explorers growing up in the digital age, technology becomes a playful ally in the foraging quest. Apps like "PlantSnap" transform the identification process into a fun and interactive game. Point your device's camera at a plant, snap a photo, and let the app work its magic. It's like having a digital companion who whispers the secrets of each green resident in the bush. Turn your foraging excursion into a high-tech treasure hunt, where every plant is a clue waiting to be deciphered.

## COMMON EDIBLE PLANTS FOR YOUR BUSHCRAFTING EXPLORATION

Let's examine the delightful world of common edible plants – nature's buffet that beckons adventurous taste buds. These abundant and easily recognizable plants make them perfect additions to your foraging repertoire.

- **Dandelions**

Picture the sunny face of a dandelion, and you've found one of the most versatile green treasures. Every part of the dandelion is edible, from the cheerful yellow flowers to the tender leaves and robust roots. Add the petals to salads, sauté the leaves as greens, or even brew tea from the roots.

Dandelions are not just common; they are nutritional powerhouses, offering young foragers a range of vitamins and minerals.

- **Clovers**

Another popular edible plant you can find in your Bushcrafting exploration is the Clover.

These seemingly ubiquitous plants are not just charming but high in protein, vitamins, and minerals. Munch on clover leaves as a crunchy snack, or add them to your salad for freshness. Nature's buffet extends beyond the conventional, and clovers invite you to explore the less-travelled paths of culinary discovery.

- **Burdock Plant**

Burdock is another edible plant you can find in the wild. It is commonly found in the North American region and is one of the ingredients in the original root beer.

While many people assume it is not edible and consider it an unwanted weed, Burdock is rich in fiber and can be boiled or roasted before eaten.

- **Wild Chicory**

This plant looks like a dandelion but with a twist! The Chicory has a tall, woody-like flower stalk reaching over four feet. You can spot it in North America with its pale blue to purple blossoms along roadsides in spring.

The leaves are edible, especially when they're young and tender. Try them raw, or if you're feeling adventurous, boil them to make them less bitter.

- **Plantain**

Found in meadows across North America, this green buddy is easily recognized. You can munch on all raw plantain parts, but it's even better when boiled. The seeds are fair game, too, raw or cooked. Just like the dandelion, plantain is high in iron and other cool vitamins and minerals.

**Note:** This plant is also called Plantago and differs from the common plantain you probably know about previously.

- **Amaranth**

Amaranth, or Pigweed, is a favorite in Indian and African diets, packed with folic acid, protein, and many other good things.

Pigweed loves to sprout early in spring; you can find it all over North America. Munch on its tender leaves raw or boiled into a tasty soup. The seeds are also a treat—try them raw, roasted, or ground into flour. It's like a tiny treasure chest of nutrition!

- **Purslane**

This is a low-growing, succulent-like wonder often overlooked. Don't let its small size fool you; it's a nutrition powerhouse! Before you snack on it, make sure you can tell it apart from its look-alike, the "hairy-stemmed purge". You can enjoy purslane raw or boiled with other herbs. It's rich in omega-3 fatty acids and has natural antibacterial powers.

- **Wood Sorrel**

You might find wood sorrel in shady spots with moist soil—a plant with a mild flavor like a hint of citrus. Every part of wood sorrel is fair game—eat it raw, mix it with other wild buddies, boil it, or turn it into a tasty tea. It's like nature's refreshing snack just waiting or you!

So, young bushcrafters, keep an eye out for these wild treats the next time you're out exploring. They're not just plants; they're your buddies in the great outdoors, ready to add a dash of adventure to your snacks!

While the bush is adorned with edible treasures, it also hides cautionary tales in the form of toxic plants. An example is the red and white amanita mushrooms, which are visually striking but potentially lethal in the wild. Young foragers must grasp the importance of distinguishing between edible delights and potentially harmful residents of the bush.

Amidst the lush greenery, instill this golden rule in your heart – never eat any plant unless you are 100% sure it's safe. The consequences of ingesting toxic plants can be severe, and it's better to err on the side of caution. Whenever you're in doubt, it's wiser to go without. A sense of responsibility and mindfulness should accompany the thrill of foraging.

Understanding the ecosystem provides additional clues to a plant's identity and characteristics. This holistic approach transforms foraging into a comprehensive educational experience, where every green treasure becomes a lesson in ecology and botany.

## CULINARY CREATIVITY: FROM IDENTIFICATION TO CREATION

As you become adept at plant identification, it is now time to unleash your culinary creativity. Experiment with recipes incorporating foraged ingredients – dandelion petal salads, clover-infused teas, or dishes inspired by other edible treasures discovered in the bush. The journey from identification to creation transforms foraging from a survival skill into a culinary art form.

As you continue to explore the bush and recognize edible plants, envision the bush as a treasure trove filled with green delights and cautionary tales. With books as guides and apps as playmates, young foragers navigate this vibrant landscape, learning to distinguish between the delectable and the dangerous. As you embark on your foraging quests, may every green treasure you encounter be a step toward culinary discovery and ecological understanding. Happy foraging, young culinary adventurers! May your bush explorations be filled with both joy and wisdom.

## FORAGING FOR INSECTS - TINY PROTEIN POWERHOUSES

Another important part of bushcraft is insects. Insects, often overlooked, are culinary treasures rich in protein, consumed in many cultures worldwide. Let's embark on a journey where mealworms become crunchy delights, crickets transform into versatile ingredients, and the bush unfolds as a pantry of tiny protein powerhouses.

- **Mealworms**

Picture mealworms as the nuts of the insect world. These larvae can be cooked and eaten, offering a crunchy texture and a nutty flavor.

Imagine adding mealworms to your culinary repertoire – a playful twist transforming ordinary dishes into extraordinary creations. These tiny morsels are delicious and nutritional powerhouses, introducing a new dimension to your foraging adventure.

- **Crickets**

Crickets, with their distinctive chirps, are not just nature's musicians but versatile ingredients in the culinary symphony. From cricket flour, a protein-rich alternative, to whole roasted crickets, these insects add a savory and nutty undertone to our dishes.

- **Grasshoppers**

Grasshoppers can often be found in grassy areas and are rich in protein. Catch them if you can, and roast or fry them for a crunchy snack.

With a hint of nutty flavor, grasshoppers are the champions of the insect world regarding taste and nutrition.

- **Termites**

Termites, the architects of the insect world, also are a chewy delight!

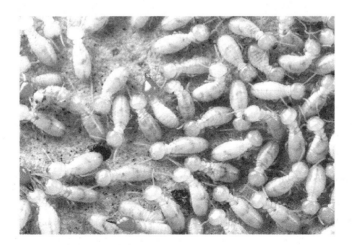

Found in decaying wood, these little insects are surprisingly high in protein. Roast them gently for a crispy texture, or munch on them as is. Termites add a woodsy flavor to your wild snacking experience.

- **Dragonflies**

Have you ever thought of turning dragonflies into a snack? These aerial acrobats are not just fascinating to watch but also edible! Found near water sources, dragonflies offer a protein-packed treat. Fry or roast them for a crispy texture, turning your bushcraft adventure into a daring culinary escapade.

- **Silkworm Pupae**

Silkworm pupae are here to surprise your taste buds! Commonly enjoyed in some cultures, these little larvae are a protein powerhouse. Boil or roast them for a unique texture and nutty taste. Silkworm pupae are a silky addition to your edible insect exploration.

There are many other edible insects in the bush. You can lay your hands on any book dedicated to these insects to learn more. But remember, do not eat it if you're not 100 per cent sure it is edible.

## CAUTIONS AMIDST THE CULINARY EXCITEMENT

While insects offer a world of culinary excitement, you must take caution as you interact with them and forage for food in the wild. Not all insects are safe to eat, and young foragers must navigate this edible landscape with prudence.

Bees, wasps, and other stinging insects are not considered part of the culinary repertoire. Their evil nature makes them unsuitable for consumption, and it's essential to avoid these buzzing creatures during foraging expeditions. The sweet reward of honey does not justify the risk of stinging insects.

Nature often communicates through color, and vibrant hues serve as warning signs in the insect world. Brightly colored insects, like some caterpillars or beetles, may be toxic if consumed. Always be on the lookout for these cautionary palettes and understand that not all colorful critters are meant to be part of their culinary explorations.

## SUPERVISION AND PROPER PREPARATION: KEYS TO SAFE FORAGING

Foraging for insects is an exciting venture, but it comes with responsibilities. Kids should always be supervised during insect foraging to ensure their safety. Additionally, proper preparation is a non-negotiable step in the culinary journey. Cooking insects thoroughly is essential not only for enhancing flavors but also for eliminating potential parasites. A well-prepared insect dish is a testament to culinary skill and a commitment to safety.

Foraging for insects extends beyond the plate, becoming an educational expedition into entomology and ecology. Teach young foragers about the ecological roles of insects, their importance in pollination, and the delicate balance they maintain within ecosystems. As they explore the culinary delights of insects, they simultaneously become stewards of the environment, understanding the interconnected web of life.

As you progress in your exploration of foraging for insects, envision it as a culinary adventure guided by cautionary wisdom. Mealworms and crickets, once seen as critters, transform into tiny protein powerhouses, adding a new dimension to your bush explorations. As you embark on this culinary journey, may every crunchy bite be a celebration of both flavor and responsibility.

## FORAGING ETHICS AND SAFETY - RESPECT AND RESPONSIBILITY

As we continue our journey into the intricate world of foraging, it's time to look into the principles of respect and responsibility that ensure our adventures positively impact the environment.

Foraging is not just a personal exploration; it's a dance with nature, a delicate partnership where respect becomes the guiding principle. As young foragers, you step into a world where every plant, insect, and creature plays a role. Teach the ethos of "leave no trace" – the idea that your presence should be like a passing breeze, leaving nature untouched and flourishing.

Imagine the bush as a banquet table, offering a feast of green treasures. However, when interacting with nature, only take what you need. Nature is generous, but it's our responsibility to ensure that the banquet table remains bountiful for all creatures, both big and small.

MINIMIZE ENVIRONMENTAL IMPACT: TREAD LIGHTLY

Foraging is a dance with the environment, and every step should be gentle. Endeavor to minimize your impact by adopting practices such as not pulling up the entire plant. The plant is a source of sustenance for us and a home and food for other creatures. Treading lightly ensures that the bush remains a vibrant ecosystem, undisturbed by our explorations.

- **Supervision by an Adult: The Guardian's Presence**

Every foraging expedition should have a guardian's watchful eye. Ensure you have an adult around when exploring the bush to provide a guiding presence that combines wisdom with a love for exploration. This supervision ensures safety and transforms foraging into a shared adventure, fostering a bond between generations.

- **Clean Hands, Clean Food: A Lesson in Hygiene**

In the bush, cleanliness is not just a virtue; it's a safety measure. Always wash your hands before and after foraging; proper hygiene is essential for bush crafting. The bush may be teeming with wonders, but cleanliness ensures that the only stories brought back are those of adventure, not of avoidable mishaps.

- **Safe Foraged Food: A Culinary Commitment**

Foraging is not just about gathering; it's about transforming the harvest into delightful meals. Teach young foragers the importance of cleaning foraged food properly before consuming it. A thorough cleaning ensures that the culinary adventure is both safe and delicious.

- **Stay Cautious**

In the bush, uncertainty is a cautionary sign. Remind young foragers never to eat anything they are unsure about. A sense of responsibility should accompany the thrill of discovery. It's wiser to err on caution, ensuring every foraged bite is a step into known and safe culinary territory.

Nature's bounty is vast, but not all corners of the bush are safe. Avoid foraging near roads or industrial areas, where pollutants might contaminate plants. The bush is a sanctuary, and our responsibility is to ensure that the treasures it offers are pure and untarnished.

As we conclude our exploration of foraging ethics and safety, remember, as young foragers, you are guardians of respect and responsibility. In the dance with nature, respect ensures that every step is harmonious, and responsibility ensures the safety of each foraging adventure. May your foraging journeys be guided by joy and wisdom, young guardians of the bush.

# SPARKING SURVIVAL - MASTERING THE ART OF FIRE CREATION AND SAFETY

Welcome, young adventurers, to a chapter that ignites the flame of survival skills in the heart of the bush. In this transformative journey, we dig into the age-old art of kindling fire, a skill that transcends practicality and becomes a beacon of warmth, protection, and a connection to the primal essence of the wilderness.

As we step into the heart of fire creation, envision the bush as a landscape and a living entity with a fiery heartbeat. Fire, a companion to humanity throughout history, transforms the wilderness into a place of warmth, light, and communal gathering. In this chapter, the flickering flames become storytellers, weaving tales of survival, camaraderie, and the symbiotic dance between humans and the untamed.

Fire is more than a tool for cooking and warmth; it symbolizes resilience and mastery over the elements. As young explorers, you are about to unlock the secrets of kindling fire, discovering its profound role in survival. The dance of flames reflects our ability to adapt, learn, and conquer challenges, echoing the spirit of our ancestors who harnessed fire to illuminate the darkness.

In the following pages, we embark on a journey into the art of fire creation – a primal skill that beckons you to become the architects of warmth amid the wild. Imagine crafting fire not just as a practical necessity but as an art form, where every kindling becomes a stroke on the canvas of survival. From the initial spark to the crackling blaze, you'll learn to coax fire into existence, becoming masters of this elemental dance.

We'll explore safe and fun fire-starting techniques. Each method becomes a lesson in skill and responsibility, emphasizing the joy of creation while instilling a deep respect for the power of fire. As you master the techniques, envision fire as a tool and a companion in your bush adventures. This guardian requires understanding and careful tending.

This chapter emphasizes the presence of guardians – adult supervision. Fire creation is a skill that requires both knowledge and responsibility. Adults become mentors, guiding young fire starters through the process while instilling the importance of respect for nature. The flames become a shared event, a symbol of collaboration between generations in the quest for survival wisdom.

Fire creation is not just a mechanical skill; it's a lesson in respect for nature. Teach young adventurers that the wood gathered is not just fuel; it's part of the ecosystem. Emphasize leaving no trace, ensuring that the beauty of the bush remains untarnished by our survival endeavors. The flames become symbols of warmth and responsibility, flickering reminders of our role as stewards of the wild.

# SPARKING SURVIVAL - MASTERING THE ART OF FIRE CREATION ...

As we journey through the pages of "Sparking Survival," envision yourselves as young fire tenders, guardians of the flame in the heart of the bush. Ignite not just the firewood but also the curiosity within you. Every spark becomes a question, every flame a story waiting to be told. Fire creation is a skill that transcends the practical; it's a dance with the elements, a connection to the primal, and a celebration of the indomitable spirit of the young explorer.

## IGNITING INTEREST - WHY FIRE IS FUNDAMENTAL IN SURVIVAL SITUATIONS

Picture the cold winds biting through the bush, and now imagine the warmth of a crackling fire fending off the chill. In survival situations, especially in cold conditions, fire emerges as a guardian against hypothermia, a silent threat that claims lives. Beyond its visual allure, fire becomes a lifeline, preserving body heat and offering a shield against the relentless cold. The flames become warmth and a safeguard against nature's icy grip.

In survival, sustenance is not just about filling the stomach; it's about transforming raw food into nourishment through the alchemy of fire. Fire serves as a culinary companion, making food safe to eat and enhancing its flavors. Imagine the aroma of a meal cooked over an open flame, a sensory delight that lifts spirits in challenging situations. The crackling of the fire becomes the rhythm of a culinary symphony, boosting morale and transforming survival into a shared feast.

Fire is more than a utilitarian tool; it's a source of comfort and a morale booster. As the flames dance and the embers glow, they weave a tapestry of light and warmth that transcends the physical. In the wilderness, where challenges abound, the comfort of a fire becomes a psychological anchor. It's a companion that whispers tales of resilience, a source of solace in the face of adversity. The fire becomes a friend, offering heat and a comforting presence in the vast unknown.

Around the campfire, stories come to life, creating a timeless tradition that spans generations. The glow of flames becomes the backdrop for campfire chronicles, where tales of adventure, wisdom, and camaraderie unfold. In the wilderness, storytelling becomes a form of entertainment and companionship, connecting the present to the echoes of the past. The crackling fire becomes the storyteller's accomplice, casting shadows that dance to the rhythm of narratives.

Also, a well-built fire, sending plumes of smoke into the sky, transforms into a signal visible for miles. In the daytime, the smoke becomes a call for assistance, an attention-grabbing plea that breaks the silence of the wild. As night falls, the glow of the fire becomes a navigational aid, guiding rescuers to lost souls in need of salvation.

See the flames from your lit fire as a practical tool but as a multifaceted companion in the wild. The dance of fire extends beyond the warmth it provides; it's a lifeline, a culinary maestro, a comforter, a storyteller. As you embark on your journey of fire mastery, may the flames be a source of survival and a timeless ally in the vast canvas of the wilderness. Happy fire crafting, young luminaries of the bush! May your flames burn bright in both the practical and poetic domains of the wild.

## FIRE STARTING 101 - SAFE AND KID-FRIENDLY TECHNIQUES

From striking sparks with magnesium fire starters to turning science into fire-making magic and, finally, discovering the treasures of nature as fire-starting aids, each technique becomes a portal to the enchanting world of fire mastery.

### MAGNESIUM FIRE STARTER

Let's start with magnesium fire starters, a reliable and safe method to strike the spark that brings fire to life. Imagine holding the power of fire in your hands with tools like the *Friendly Swede Magnesium Alloy Emergency Fire Starter Blocks*. These compact wonders are easy to use and resilient in wet conditions, making them ideal companions for your bush escapades.

You can take charge by scraping the magnesium block with a knife or striker to ignite the spark. As the magnesium shavings rain down, a shower of sparks is born, ready to dance with the tinder. It's a tactile and exciting method that teaches fire-starting skills and instils empowerment as you learn to create fire from the raw elements.

### BATTERY AND STEEL WOOL MAGIC

Our next technique transforms fire-starting into an electrifying experiment. Under the watchful eye of adult supervision, you can explore the basic principles of electricity while igniting a fire. All that's needed is a standard Energizer 9-volt battery and steel wool.

Touch the steel wool to the battery's terminals and witness the magic unfold. The electrical current coursing through the steel wool causes it to glow and ignite. It's a captivating experiment that not only ignites fires but sparks curiosity about the wonders of science.

## NATURE'S BOUNTY: GATHERING TINDER FROM THE WILDERNESS

Our final technique takes us on a nature walk, transforming the wilderness into a treasure trove of fire-starting materials. Dry grass, pine needles, and bark shavings become the natural tinder that ignites the flames. This activity teaches practical fire-starting skills, enhances a child's observation abilities, and deepens their connection to the environment.

Imagine the joy of exploring the outdoors, gathering materials for the fire-starting adventure. Every piece of dry grass becomes a potential flame, and each pine needle holds the promise of a crackling fire. It's a hands-on lesson in resourcefulness and an opportunity for young adventurers to understand their natural surroundings better.

As we conclude this exploration of fire starting, see yourselves as young fire crafters armed with the knowledge of safe and kid-friendly techniques. Magnesium fire starters, electrifying experiments, and nature's bounty become your tools in the quest for fire mastery. May your flames burn bright, young fire apprentices, illuminating not just the bush but also the paths of curiosity and exploration that lie ahead.

## FIRE SAFETY FOR YOUNG EXPLORERS

It's paramount to understand that fire is a powerful tool, not a toy, and with great power comes great responsibility. In this part of the book, we emphasize the vital role of adult supervision, the art of keeping fires contained, and the profound importance of respecting nature through "Leave No Trace" principles.

- **Adult Supervision**

No matter the method used to conjure the flames, adult supervision is the cornerstone of fire safety. Adults are not just mentors but guardians, ensuring that safety guidelines are adhered to and stepping in if situations become hazardous. Emphasize to young explorers that fire, while a captivating ally, demands respect and caution. It's a tool that requires wisdom, and adult supervision ensures that the flames dance within safety boundaries.

- **Fire is a Tool, Not a Toy**

A crucial lesson awaits in the enchanting dance of flames – fire is a tool, not a toy. Misuse can lead to serious consequences, and young fire apprentices must understand the responsibility of wielding this elemental force. Remind them that every spark they create carries the weight of both opportunity and accountability. Fire becomes a companion only when treated with the respect it deserves.

- **Keeping Fires Contained**

The next lesson takes us to the practical aspect of fire safety – keeping fires contained. When in the bush, cultivate the art of building fire rings with rocks or digging fire pits, using tools like a shovel to assist in this task. These containment measures ensure the safety of the surroundings and create a designated space for the flames.

Fires should never be left unattended, a fundamental rule etched in fire safety principles. Young explorers must learn the importance of vigilance, understanding that the responsibility of tending to the fire extends from its inception to its complete extinction. Before leaving the area, every flame must be fully extinguished, leaving no room for potential hazards.

- **Respecting Nature**

In the realm of fire safety, nature is not just a backdrop; it's a partner in the adventure. Young explorers must be conscious of the potential impact of their fires on the environment. Collect only dead, fallen wood for the fires, avoiding harming living trees. This practice aligns with the "Leave No Trace" principles we mentioned earlier, ensuring the natural surroundings remain pristine.

It is essential to always fully extinguish fires after use and scatter the ashes after they've been cooled. The mark of a responsible bushcrafter is one who leaves no trace of their fiery escapades. Nature is a sanctuary, and the flames, while welcome companions, should not leave scars on the landscape. By instilling a deep respect for the environment, young explorers become stewards of the wilderness, guardians who tread lightly and leave no imprint behind.

As we conclude this journey of fire safety, envision yourselves not just as fire apprentices but as bearers of wisdom and responsibility. Adult supervision becomes the guardian's watchful eye, fire becomes a tool to be wielded with respect, containment measures ensure safety, and "Leave No Trace" principles become a creed to live by.

## FUN WITH FIRE - ENGAGING ACTIVITIES TO PRACTICE FIRE-STARTING SKILLS

As you embark on the exhilarating journey of fire mastery, this part of the book unfolds like a treasure map, guiding you through engaging activities that sharpen your fire-starting skills and transform the learning process into a thrilling adventure. From challenges that test your resourcefulness to cooking over open flames and using fire as a guide to understanding wind and weather, every activity becomes a spark that ignites your curiosity.

- **Natural Materials Challenge: The Quest for Fire**

Our first challenge echoes the primal instincts of our ancestors – starting a fire using only natural materials gathered from the wild. This activity reinforces fire-starting skills and becomes a canvas for observation and resourcefulness. You can compete among others in your expedition, sparking flames to life and reveling in the satisfaction of a skill honed through hands-on experience. It's a quest for fire that transforms learning into an adventure, testing skill and ingenuity.

The flames flicker, and the competition begins! You can compete to see who can start their fire first or keep it burning the longest. This friendly competition not only adds an element of excitement but also nurtures a sense of camaraderie among you and your fellow bushcrafters. It's a celebration of skills learned, and challenges overcome, turning the bush into a playground where sparks of ingenuity fly and flames dance with the spirit of friendly rivalry.

- **Cooking Over the Fire: A Culinary Adventure**

Now that you've been able to start your fire, this becomes a tool for a culinary escapade. You can cook a simple meal over the fire you've built, such as hot dogs or marshmallows. Cooking over an open flame is not just fun and rewarding; it's a tangible reward for your fire-starting efforts. As you savor the fruits of your labor, a valuable survival skill is ingrained – the ability to prepare a meal using the elemental force of fire. It's a culinary adventure that transforms the bush into a kitchen where every flame becomes a master chef's ally.

- **Fire as a Weather Guide: Observing Wind and Prediction**

The dance of smoke becomes a lesson in navigation and weather prediction. Observing the smoke from a fire helps you learn about wind direction, a useful skill in the wilderness. With adult guidance, you can delve into the intricacies of weather conditions – how humidity and wind speed affect fire behavior. This isn't just fire-watching; it's a journey into the art of understanding nature's cues. The flames become not just a source of warmth but also guides deciphering the elements' secrets.

As you continue your exploration of the bush, the challenges you've undertaken with your fellow bushcrafters on "fun with fire" become stepping stones, competitions become celebrations, culinary escapades become feats of survival, and fire becomes a guide to unlocking the mysteries of nature. May your flames burn bright, young explorers of the bush, illuminating not just the night sky but also the pathways of curiosity and discovery that lie ahead. Happy bushcrafting!

# RIDING THE STORM: UNDERSTANDING WEATHER IN THE WILD

We've covered many aspects of bushcrafting so far. However, in this chapter, we're diving into the world of weather. Imagine the sky as a storyteller or a fortune teller telling you what to expect in the next couple of seconds, minutes, and even hours.

Look up, and you'll see a vast canvas painted with clouds. Each cloud has its own story to tell. Fluffy white clouds? Those are the cotton candy dreamers, bringing sunshine and blue skies. Dark, brooding clouds? They're the rainmakers, ready to dance and shower the earth. Understanding clouds is like reading nature's book—each page tells a new story about what the weather might bring.

Feel that gentle breeze on your face? Or is it a strong gust tugging at your hair? That's the wind, nature's messenger! The wind carries secrets about the weather. When it whispers, it might mean fair weather ahead. But if it howls and gusts, get ready for a stormy adventure! So, pay attention to the wind's whispers—it's nature's way of chatting with you.

Have you ever danced in the rain? Raindrops are like nature's drumbeats, creating a rhythmic melody on leaves and rooftops. When rain joins the adventure, it brings life to the land. But not all rain is the same. Some showers are soft and gentle, while others might be fierce and loud. Each raindrop has a story to tell, and by listening, you can understand what kind of rain is tapping on your window.

Suppose you are in the bush and hear a boom! That might be thunder and the flash of light. Lightning! When thunder and lightning join the party, it's like nature putting on a spectacular fireworks show. Thunder is the sound of lightning dancing across the sky. Count the seconds between the flash and the boom to know how far away the storm is. If it's close, find shelter and enjoy the show from a safe spot!

Ever wanted to be a weather wizard? You can! Keep an eye on the sky, listen to the wind, and feel the air. If the clouds gather and the wind starts to get loud, a storm might be brewing. But if the sun smiles and the birds are chirping, get ready for a sun-soaked adventure. Understanding the weather is all about observing and being in sync with nature's mood.

Different weathers have their telltale signs when we look up at the sky, and as young bushcrafters, you will learn to identify and manage yourselves in whatever you might find yourself in your bushcrafting exploration. So, get ready to ride the storm as we unravel the mysteries of weather in the wild!

## CLOUDY WITH A CHANCE OF ADVENTURE: RECOGNIZING BASIC WEATHER PATTERNS

The first step to understanding the weather is to learn the secrets of basic weather patterns. Imagine the atmosphere as a grand puzzle, and together, let us decipher the language of clouds, wind, rain, thunder, and lightning. Get ready for a weather adventure like no other!

## THE CLOUDY CAST: CLOUD TYPES AND THEIR MEANINGS

If you look up sometimes, you might witness a vast sky painted with various cloud characters. Each of these cloud types has its uniqueness and often serves as a pointer to the kind of weather that's brewing. Let's look at these clouds and see what they are telling us about the weather.

- **Cumulus Clouds - The Cotton Candy Puffs**

On bright and sunny days, you'll often spot cumulus clouds dotting the sky. These fluffy, white clouds resemble cotton candy, floating lazily and promising hours of outdoor fun. When cumulus clouds are around, you can count on fair weather and clear skies.

- **Cirrus Clouds - Wispy High-Fliers**

If you see wispy or thin clouds high above, almost like feathers delicately painted on a blue canvas, these are cirrus clouds, and they often signal changes in the weather. When cirrus clouds make an appearance, it's a gentle reminder that the atmosphere might witness a weather change soon.

- **Nimbostratus and Cumulonimbus Clouds - Rainmakers and Thunderstorm Creators**

The two types of clouds that often instill panic in the mind of adventurers are the nimbostratus and the cumulonimbus clouds because they signal rain and thunderstorms. Nimbostratus clouds bring with them steady rainfall, turning the sky into a gray masterpiece. When you see nimbostratus clouds, it's time to grab your umbrella. On the other hand, cumulonimbus clouds are the precursors of thunderstorms. They are often towering clouds with an anvil-like top—these bring lightning, thunder, and intense rain. It's nature's way of adding a bit of excitement to the sky.

## UNDERSTANDING THE SECRET LANGUAGE OF THE WIND

The wind is like a whispering friend. It carries with it tales of the atmosphere. Understanding its language is like decoding nature's secret messages. Wind generally flows from areas of high pressure to low pressure, creating a beautiful dance in the sky. You can use a simple weathervane or watch the rustling leaves to understand what the wind is trying to tell you. Knowing wind directions helps you predict changes in the weather and adds an exciting element to your outdoor adventures.

## UNDERSTANDING DIFFERENT LEVELS OF RAIN

Raindrops aren't just wet surprises; each drop and its intensity are trying to pass a message across. Let's try to understand these levels of rain and what they are telling us.

- **Light Rain**

If you see soft, steady rain falling from the sky, it's like nature's way of giving the plants a refreshing drink. When light rain graces the day, it's the perfect time for cozy indoor activities or a quiet read. Therefore, if you're in the bush, you can enjoy the company of your fellow bushcrafters as you all cozy up together in your camp setup. Also, if you're up to the task, you can walk around for a bit in the rain. However, ensure you don't stay too long in the rain, so you don't become feverish.

- **Heavy Rain**

On the other hand, when rain comes down hard and fast, it's a sign that a storm is ready to put on a show. Get ready to cozy up indoors, listen to the rhythmic drumming of raindrops, and enjoy the sound of rain tapping on your window.

- **Thunder and Lightning**

When this duo joins the party, it's like nature putting on a spectacular fireworks show. Thunder and lightning create a dynamic drumroll and flash show in the sky—exciting but best enjoyed from the safety of indoors.

If you want to get better at recognizing and understanding the weather, you can start your very own weather journal. Note down what the sky looks like, how the wind behaves, and whether raindrops are tap-dancing or pouring. Over time, you would have created a weather diary that helps you understand the patterns in your surroundings. Your journal becomes a treasure trove of weather wisdom, and you might even discover your inner meteorologist!

By recognizing these basic weather patterns, you've taken the first step in understanding the sky's language. Clouds, wind, rain, thunder, and lightning—they're not just elements in the sky; they're your friends in decoding nature's mood. So, put on your bushcrafting exploration hat, grab your journal, and let the atmospheric adventure continue.

## WEATHERING THE ELEMENTS: PREPARING FOR DIFFERENT WEATHER CONDITIONS

As you continue your journey in the fascinating world of bushcrafting, and you start to understand the weather, you must also learn to prepare yourself for whatever weather you might find yourself. Mother Nature loves surprises, and understanding how to weather the elements ensures that you're always prepared for whatever she throws your way. Therefore, in this section of the book, we will explore how to navigate rain, shine, wind, and storms with confidence.

## RAINY DAYS

Rainy days can be magical if you're prepared to embrace them. It's like nature's way of giving the Earth a big, refreshing hug. Here's how you can make the most of a rainy day:

- **Rain Gear**

Invest in a raincoat, a sturdy umbrella, and waterproof boots. With the right gear, you can dance, jump in puddles, and explore the wonders of a rain-soaked bush without getting soaked. The amazing thing about rain gear is that even when you're out of the bush and in the city, they are also handy and can keep you from getting wet or getting feverish.

- **Indoor Adventures**

When the rain is pouring down, shift your adventures indoors. Board games, puzzles, and reading become extra cozy on a rainy day. Therefore, even though you're going bushcrafting, always bring fun games along for times like this. You can also get creative with arts and crafts to bring a bit of sunshine to the gloom.

## SUNNY DAYS

When the sun is shining brightly, it's time for outdoor fun, but staying cool is the key. Here's how to beat the heat like a pro:

- **Sunscreen**

Before stepping out of your campground or house, apply sunscreen to protect your skin from the sun's powerful rays. A hat and sunglasses are also excellent sidekicks to keep you cool and stylish.

- **Hydration**

Keep a water bottle by your side to stay hydrated. Water is essential for hot days in and out of the bush. Whether you're on your bushcrafting journey, within the city, playing sports, going for a nature walk, or simply lounging in the backyard, water is your best friend on sunny days and not just in the bush.

## WINDY WEATHER

Windy days add a touch of excitement to the air. Here's how to make the most of them:

- **Wind-Friendly Fun**

Fly a kite, let bubbles dance in the wind, or try your hand at making wind chimes. Windy days are perfect for activities that harness the power of the breeze.

- **Hold Onto Your Hat**

If the wind is extra strong, make sure your hat is securely fastened. Otherwise, your hat might fly off your head like a kite, and you might have a hard time finding it in the bush.

## STORMY DAYS

Thunderstorms bring their brand of drama to the weather stage. Here's how to stay safe and sound:

- **Indoor Retreat**

When thunder roars, head back to your rendezvous point or campground and meet with the rest of your bushcraft. Find a cozy spot and enjoy the storm from the safety of your camp tent. Bring out board games or a good book to make it an indoor adventure.

- **Emergency Kit Essentials**

Before embarking on your bushcrafting journey, ensure you prepare a simple emergency kit with essentials like a flashlight, snacks, and a cozy blanket. Having these items on hand adds a touch of comfort during stormy weather.

- **Thunder Clap Countdown**

When counting the seconds between a lightning flash and the thunderclap, every five seconds means that the storm is about one mile away. This trick helps you keep track of how close (or far) the storm is.

By mastering the art of weathering the elements, you're equipped to face raindrops, sunshine, breezy days, and storms with confidence. Remember, each weather condition is an opportunity for a new adventure. So, whether you're dancing in the rain, soaking up the sun, riding the breeze, or staying cozy during a storm, embrace the magic of every moment and enjoy your bushcrafting adventures to the fullest.

## UNDER COVER: BUILDING WEATHER-RESISTANT SHELTERS

Whether you're in the bush or the city, you'll undoubtedly face different kinds of weather. In that case, it is essential to ensure that your bushcraft shelter can withstand different kinds of weather. Sometimes, you might need to be sheltered from cold; sometimes, it might be rain or storm. You need a shelter that can withstand these different weathers. Each season and environment brings its unique challenges, but certain universal principles govern the creation of wilderness survival shelters. So, let's look at some checklists to put in place to ensure your shelter is as weather-resistant as possible.

## LOCATION: THE KEYSTONE OF SHELTER CRAFTING

The first factor you must consider when constructing your shelter is location. Your choice of location can significantly increase or drastically reduce your chance of getting the optimal shelter that can resist different weather challenges. An ideal location satisfies two critical criteria:

- **Access to Building Materials:**

Choose a spot offering easy access to abundant building materials like sticks, leaves, grasses, etc. Proximity to such resources streamlines the construction process. However, be careful you don't choose a spot close to "widowmakers." Widowmakers are trees or branches that are in the process of dying as they might fall anytime and crash your shelter. Also, while you don't want water pooling around your shelter, proximity to a water source for convenience is advantageous. However, be mindful of potential risks, especially when it's raining.

- **Hazard Avoidance**

Steer clear of significant hazards such as falling branches, pooling water, and insect nests. Ensure your shelter is located in a spot that's shielded from prevailing winds to safeguard against the elements. Opt for a location with a sufficiently flat area, providing comfort for lying down and sleeping. Also, you must avoid areas frequented by wildlife, respect their paths and living spaces to ensure a safe and undisturbed shelter.

## MAKE A PLAN

A well-thought-out plan saves energy and streamlines the building process. Before commencing construction, survey the environment and determine the required shelter type, size, and location. Pause, breathe, and contemplate, ensuring your plan aligns with the surrounding resources and your protection needs.

A common pitfall that many first-time and inexperienced bushcrafters fall into is building huge shelters. Not only does this demand more materials and effort, but it can result in a colder interior due to the increased space. Effective wilderness shelters are often small and precisely sized to accommodate your body and conserve body heat.

Also, you must prioritize your safety when constructing your shelter. Make use of large, robust branches to form the initial framework, ensuring they can bear your weight. This is especially critical for lean-to and debris hut-style shelters.

## INSULATION AND COVER

Regardless of the environment, insulation and cover are essential to shield against external elements. Starting from the ground up, insulating materials are crucial for creating a cozy shelter.

- **Ground Insulation:**

Use natural substances like dead leaves, pine needles, or bark to cushion the ground. If available, incorporate a sleeping bag, pad, or emergency blanket into your plan for enhanced insulation.

- **Wall and Roof Insulation:**

Once the shelter frame is established, insulate the walls and roof by adding layers of debris, such as leaves and pine needles. The thicker the insulation, the better your shelter will protect against the cold.

## BUILD A STABLE SHELTER FRAME

The frame of your shelter provides its structural foundation. So, it is a no-brainer that you must pay special attention to ensuring the frame is sturdy enough to withstand forces from weather like wind or storm.

- **Foundation**

Construct the shelter against a natural element like a tree or boulder. Begin with a long, solid piece of wood forming the shelter's spine. Use wood that is slightly longer than your height to ensure your comfort.

- **Wall and Roof Structure**

For common shelter types like *lean-to* or *A-frame* that we mentioned in Chapter 2, the roof is integrated into the walls. Use sturdy sticks at a 45-degree angle against the spine to create a rib cage-like structure. Add branches with offshoots as shingles to form the roof.

# RIDING THE STORM: UNDERSTANDING WEATHER IN THE WILD

Lay long, thick sticks along the spine, forming a tight rib cage for stability, and secure branches with offshoots along the walls, resembling shingles. These also provide extra stability for the insulation.

## CONSIDER YOUR HEAT SOURCE

In cold environments, preventing hypothermia becomes a primary concern. Bushcraft shelters offer two primary choices for a heat source:

- **Body Heat**

If you want your shelter to rely on body heat, then it should be compact, with enough insulating debris to mimic the warmth of a sleeping bag. Think of it as creating a mummy sleeping bag with extra insulation.

## DRESS FOR SUCCESS: WEATHER-APPROPRIATE CLOTHING AND GEAR

In your bushcraft exploration, dressing appropriately for the weather is as important as building the right shelter. The right gear can make a big difference in comfort and safety.

For example, in hot weather, you will be better off with loose, light-colored clothes to keep you cool and a wide-brimmed hat to protect you from the sun. While in the cold weather, several layers of clothing can provide better insulation than one thick layer.

Also, in the rain, waterproof clothing and footwear are essential. Just like knights have their armor and wizards their wands, bush crafters have their set of essentials to conquer the elements.

Therefore, let's learn about weather-appropriate clothing and gear to ensure that you're dressed for success in your bushcrafting quest!

## STAYING PROTECTED FROM THE SUN

When the sun is beaming down, some of the gear and clothing that can keep you protected include:

- **Sunscreen Shields**

Before stepping out into the sunny wild, apply sunscreen to keep your skin protected. Choose a sunscreen with a high SPF to shield your skin from the sun's rays. This essential outdoor gear helps prevent sunburns and keeps your skin happy.

- **Hats**

A trusty hat is essential for protecting your face and neck from the sun's powerful gaze. Choose a wide-brimmed hat for maximum shade, and you'll be ready to face the sun with confidence.

## GEARING UP FOR RAINY DAYS

For the times when your bushcrafting adventure becomes rain-filled, here are some gears to keep you protected from the rain:

- **Waterproof Jackets**

Equip yourself with a waterproof jacket or poncho. This helps you repel raindrops and keeps you dry and cozy. This essential piece of clothing ensures that rainy days are merely a splash of fun, not a soaking adventure.

- **Boots**

The ground may turn into puddle-filled moats during rainstorms. In Times like this, what you need for your feet is waterproof boots —sturdy guardians that keep your toes dry and help you conquer wet and wild terrains.

- **Windbreaker Shields**

The rain often comes with winds. However, sometimes, the wind might come on its own. In such cases, a windbreaker jacket is your trusty shield against the breeze. Lightweight and resistant, it keeps the wind at bay while allowing you to move freely.

- **Emergency Shelter Kit**

For unforeseen storms, carry a compact emergency shelter kit. This may include a lightweight tarp, paracord, and stakes. With this kit, you can quickly create a makeshift shelter (remember you've learned how to make weather-resistant shelters) to weather the storm safely.

As you learn how to dress for success in different weather conditions, you've taken a further step towards having a swell bushcrafting experience. Whether you're in the sun's warm embrace, dancing in the rain, taming the wind, or confronting mighty storms, your weather-appropriate clothing and gear are your trusty companions. So, gear up, brave bushcrafters, and let the wilderness become your runway.

## WHEN WEATHER STRIKES: SAFETY MEASURES DURING EXTREME WEATHER

There are times in your bushcrafting journey when you might experience extreme weather conditions. Severe weather can be dangerous, but knowing what to do can help keep you safe. By understanding safety measures during these challenging moments, you'll be well-equipped to navigate the wilderness with confidence and resilience. So, let's look at measures to take when extreme weather strikes.

- **Thunderstorm**

During thunderstorms, it's crucial to find shelter. Avoid open areas and tall, isolated trees-they're lightning's favorite spot to strike. If you can't find shelter, crouching low in a bushy area is safer than standing tall. Lightning seeks the highest point, and you want to stay as low as possible.

- **Snowstorm**

When you're facing a snowstorm, staying dry is your shield against the cold. Build a shelter to protect yourself from the swirling snowflakes and keep a fire going for warmth. A roaring fire can be your winter companion, ensuring you don't develop hypothermia.

- **Heatwaves**

When the sun turns up the heat, you need enough water to conquer the excess heat. Stay cool by drinking water regularly, even before you feel thirsty. Thirst is a sign that dehydration has already begun, so take sips throughout the day. Also, take regular breaks from your adventure and find refuge under a tree or create your shady oasis.

Armed with these safety measures, you're prepared to triumph over nature's extreme weather. Whether you're coursing through a thunderstorm, navigating a snowstorm, or beating the heat, you've equipped yourself with the secrets to conquering any weather. So, go forth with confidence, face nature's challenges head-on, and emerge victorious in every weather quest. Always remember that the key to staying safe is to be alert at all times, remain prepared, and respect nature's power.

# BAND-AIDS AND BRAVERY: FIRST AID BASICS FOR LITTLE EXPLORERS

Imagine a situation where you cut your leg on a tree stump because you did not notice it on time. You feel your leg hit something, and it sends the pain throughout your body. You bend quickly to examine the wound, and you notice there's blood at the spot where you hit your leg. If you do not know first aid, you might panic at that point. What's worse is that if you don't take proper care of such a cut, it might develop into something much more serious. That is why you need to learn about first aid and first aid kits before you embark on your bushcrafting journey through the wild.

First aid is like a superhero's toolkit for little explorers, a magical skill set that transforms scraped knees and minor mishaps into stories of triumph. It's the knowledge that you can apply to mend bruises and little accidents you might encounter in your exploration.

To perform first aid, you'll also need to have a first aid kit. It's a miniature arsenal containing Band-Aids, antiseptic wipes, and soothing creams; each item in this kit has its unique use in the process of quick and easy treatments. The heroes of the kit are the Band-Aids, and they come adorned with whimsical designs and hold the power to mend not only cuts and scrapes but also little hearts. Antiseptic wipes stand as guardians against infection and soothing creams; the healers provide comfort to the wounded.

First aid and its trusty kit empower young adventurers to face the challenges of the wild with courage and resilience, ensuring that every outdoor escapade is a safe and magical journey. So, together, we'll explore how these items work their wonders, offering comfort and relief with a sprinkle of first aid magic.

However, with great power comes great responsibility! So, we'll look at the importance of knowledge and the guiding hand of adult supervision. Just as a seasoned explorer leads the way through unknown territories, adults will be your compass, ensuring safety and wisdom as you navigate the world of first aid.

By the end of this chapter, you'll not only be skilled in the art of giving first aid, but you'll also be brimming with confidence as a well-informed and adventure-ready bush crafter. No scrape or bruise will be too daunting, for you'll hold the key to first aid magic—a skill set that transforms every little explorer into a true hero of the wild.

## THE ABCS OF FIRST AID: UNDERSTANDING THE BASICS

First aid is more than a set of skills; it's a noble goal—to be the helping hands that make a difference. It's the immediate assistance given to someone in need, a response that can turn the tide in the face of emergencies. The essence is to preserve life, prevent conditions from worsening, and set the stage for recovery. It's the compass that guides you even in uncertain times.

In your exploration of the wild, your knowledge of first aid is the trump card. Learning first aid is not just a skill; it's a superpower that can make a significant difference in the outcome of an emergency. Whether you're navigating a forest trail or enjoying a sunny day in the city park, the wisdom of first aid transforms you into a guardian, ready to respond with care and competence.

## BYSTANDER CPR: A VITAL SKILL

As you begin to learn and understand the importance of first aid, one of the first things to know is bystander CPR (Cardio Pulmonary Resuscitation). According to the American Heart Association, effective bystander CPR, provided immediately after sudden cardiac arrest, can double or even triple a victim's chance of survival. It's a vital note in the melody of life-saving skills, a call to action that can rewrite the destiny of those in need.

Imagine a situation where one of your fellow bushcrafters suddenly develops cardiac arrest (when the heart stops). In the middle of the bush, it might take a lot of work to get prompt and timely access to healthcare. However, as a hero with the knowledge of CPR, you can quickly administer first aid to your friends and help stabilize them. So, bystander CPR is an effective first aid knowledge to equip yourself with as you explore the wild and become an excellent bushcrafter.

## HOW TO GIVE CPR

There are two things you need for an effective CPR. The first is 30 chest pump and the second thing is to give them two breaths.

- **Chest Pump**

The first thing to do when you want to give CPR is to kneel beside the person that needs the first aid. Ensure the person is lying down properly. Kneel next to them and place the heel of one hand in the middle of their chest. Now, the other hand joins in, and your fingers interlace. Straighten your elbows and start the action. When you push down, make sure your hands don't bounce. Keep the heel of your hand touching the chest.

However, if the person is younger than 8, use one hand to push down about 1.5 inches. Let the chest come back up before doing it again. Keep that rhythm going – 30 times as fast as you can.

- **The Breath of Life**

After the 30th chest pump, it is time to give *breath*. To do that, follow this checklist;

1. Make sure the airway is clear and pinch their nose to close it.
2. Use two fingers to gently lift their chin. This move is like giving their body a little wake-up call.
3. Take a deep breath, and gently place your mouth over theirs. Blow into their airway and watch their chest rise and fall. Repeat the breath routine.

Go back to the compressions – 30 times, and then another round of breaths. Follow this routine about five times, and then check if they're breathing normally.

In emergencies, CPR is essential for ensuring any accident doesn't lead to loss of lives.

## THE GUIDING PRINCIPLES: SEEKING PROFESSIONAL HELP

As you begin to learn how to administer first aid, you will start to feel a lot more confident in your ability to stabilize yourself or others around you in emergencies. However, one guiding principle of first aid is always to seek professional help when necessary. While, as a young adventurer, you can effectively and efficiently wield the tools of first aid, you should always remember the importance of alerting an adult or calling 911 in serious emergencies. It's a partnership between youthful readiness and the wisdom of experienced hands.

Always remember, first aid is not just a skill; it's a mantle of responsibility. As you grasp the ABCs of first aid, remember that knowledge is a torch, and with it, you illuminate the path to safety for yourself and those around you.

## SCRATCHES AND SCRAPES: TREATING MINOR INJURIES

Sometimes, during your bushcrafting adventure, you might walk against a thorny leave or an unsuspecting tree stub, and suddenly —bam!—you get a scratch or a scrape? Well, that's just nature's way of saying, "Hey, you're doing something exciting!"

Imagine the bush as a massive canvas and those little scratches and scrapes you pick up while exploring. They're like nature's way of giving you cool badges of courage. Each mark tells a story of how you bravely faced the wild and its awesome challenges. Therefore, instead of panicking when you get scratched or scraped, see yourself as an artist, and the wild is your art studio. The twigs and rocks? Those are your brushes. The mud and grass stains? Those are your colors. And those scratches? They're like your unique signature on a masterpiece that only you can create.

So, whenever you get scraped from a wild tumble, the first step in the healing process is to clean yourself up. Grab some clean water from a cool mountain stream for example, or from the water you've gotten for yourself to stay hydrated, and use a gentle soap. It's like giving your scrape a refreshing shower to wash away the dust.

With the cleaning done, the next part is to apply some antibiotics or ointment. This is one of the ingredients that must be a part of your First aid kit. Dab it on your scrape, and let it work its magic, protecting your skin and helping it get back to its awesome self. It's like having a superhero sidekick in the healing journey.

Next up, after applying the ointment, cover the scrape with a bandage! They're like your adventure buddies making sure no adventure dirt or germs sneak in.

So, you're not just an adventurer now; you're a superhero adventurer, complete with a healing cape! You look in the mirror, see that bandage, and think, "Yeah, I faced a wild adventure, and I conquered it like a superhero!"

## WHEN TO GET EXTRA HELP

Now, let's talk about when your scrape needs some extra attention. If it's a super deep cut, or it won't stop bleeding, or if something rusty or dirty caused it, that's when you call in the grown-up. They're mostly more experienced than you and have what it takes to handle the tougher injuries.

When you call in a more experienced grown-up to check your scrape or bruise, they'll be able to take a closer look and determine what exactly they need to do or apply to the wound to get it healed. Once they carry out the necessary treatment, you'll be firmly on your way to continue to adventure and exploration of

Remember, you're not just an adventurer; you're also responsible for keeping yourself healthy during your adventure. With each bump and scrape, you're dancing with nature, turning those marks into stories of your epic adventures. The bush is your stage, and you're the star of the show, creating a masterpiece with every step.

So, fellow adventurer, keep rocking it. You're not just fixing bumps and bruises; you're crafting stories that will be told around the campfire for generations. The bushcraft adventure continues!

## BUG BITES AND RASHES: DEALING WITH SKIN IRRITATIONS

When you're in the woods, discovering hidden trails and secret spots, and getting closer to Mother Nature, the potential injuries are not limited to bruises and scrapings. Sometimes, you might get bitten by bugs and develop rashes, or you might even innocently come in contact with itchy plants. For that reason, you must learn how to notice and deal with the itchy, scratchy, and sometimes downright annoying side of things.

- **Itchy Plants**

As you navigate through the wild, one of the plants you might come across is a plant known as the poison ivy, the sneaky trickster of the plant world. This plant is not your friend. It is the mischief-maker that can leave you with an itchy rash. But you do not need to panic. All you need is to know how to outsmart this green troublemaker.

First rule: Learn to spot poison ivy. The poison ivy is a plant with three shiny leaves, kind of like a tricky clover. If you accidentally brush against it, your first move is to run to safety. Then, give your skin a good, thorough wash with water and soap.

Now, here's the golden rule—no scratching! We know it's tough not to scratch when you get itchy, but scratching only makes the itch worse. So, endure the itch and resist the urge to scratch. If the itch is too wild, you can apply some anti-itch cream - This is another item in your first aid kit - or ask an adult to help you apply the cream. Once applied, the anti-itch cream will help you tame the itchiness.

- **Mosquitoes**

Next up on the bugs and itch lists are our tiny, buzzing rivals—the mosquitoes. These little bugs often see humans as their snack, especially when you enter their habitat to meet them, but you mustn't let them have a feast as they might infect you with malaria.

Thus, when going on bushcraft adventures, you are more likely to be protected against bugs like mosquitoes by wearing long-sleeve shirts and trousers. In addition to that, applying mosquito repellant on your skin will keep these bugs away. Imagine it as some cloak or armor that makes you invincible to mosquitoes.

But what if, despite all your defenses, a sneaky mosquito still gets a bite on you? No worries, young adventurer. Remember the anti-itch cream from earlier that will also come in handy in this situation, and the itch from the bite won't stand a chance!

What if a bite or sting causes more than just a little discomfort? If you ever feel like you're having trouble breathing or swallowing, or if things get dizzy or your heart starts racing—this is your signal to call in the grown-up ASAP as this could be a sign of something called anaphylaxis, a fancy word for a serious allergic reaction. So, remember, this is not a battle you fight alone; you've got the more experienced grown-ups by your side.

FIRST AID FOR BUG BITES AND RASHES

Outside of the plants and bugs we've mentioned so far, you might come across other bugs and plants that cause you discomfort during your bushcrafting adventure. To that end, let's look at some general steps to take and administer first aid when needed.

- **Step 1 - The Discovery and Inspection Phase:** It's a no-brainer that the very first step is for you to discover what it is that just happened to you. When you're sure of what just happened, you'll be more accurately informed to make the right decisions to salvage the situation. So, you need to examine the bite or rash. Is it a mosquito bite, a bee sting, or perhaps a plant-induced rash? Knowing your enemy helps you choose the right tools from your first aid kit.

- **Step 2 - Cleansing:** The next step is to clean the rash or bite spot with a mixture of soap and water. Gently cleanse the affected area to wash away any dirt or potential allergens. Ensure not to rub it too hard so as not to injure your skin further or peel it.

- **Step 3 - Treatment:** The next stage is where you enter the treatment proper. Here, you apply creams like hydrocortisone or calamine lotion to the spot to give some soothing effect to the itch or bite. Also, you can apply other anti-itch creams to the spot to relieve the itchiness.

- **Step 4 - Ice-pack treatment:** After applying the anti-itch cream, you can also place an ice-pack on the bite or rash if available. Leave this on the spot for about 10 minutes to reduce swelling and numb any pain you might be feeling. Once that is done, you can proceed to find a place to rest.

- **Step 5 - The Grown-Up Hero Alert:** This is the last step of your first aid. If the bite or rash seems to be spreading, getting more swollen, or causing severe discomfort—it's time to call in the grown-up. Remember, they're more experienced than you are and are there to ensure you stay safe at all times.

Now that you've completed our crash course in first aid for bug bites and rashes, you're ready to face nature's challenges like the true adventurer you are! Even though the bugs and itchy plants might try to throw you a curveball, but armed with knowledge, you're not just an explorer; you're a conqueror of nature's challenges. So, Keep your eyes sharp, your armor on, and your spirits high. Now, go out there, brave hearts, and show nature who's boss.

## HEAT AND COLD: PREVENTING DEHYDRATION AND HYPOTHERMIA

Young bushcrafters, we're gradually getting closer to becoming experts in our exploration of the wild. However, as you prepare to commence your adventure finally, there are some elements you need to learn more about and pay more attention to. These elements are dehydration from excess heat and hypothermia from excess cold. While these elements surely sound scary, fear not, little bushcrafters, together we will imbibe you with a treasure trove of knowledge to conquer these sneaky foes and emerge victorious in your bushcraft quests.

## HYDRATION STATION: OUTSMARTING DEHYDRATION

Imagine yourself deep in the heart of the wilderness, surrounded by towering trees and chirping birds. But the sun is blazing, and you're feeling a bit like a walking cactus - devoid of water. In such a situation, the solution is glaring - drink water.

Water is one of the things that should always be a part of your first aid kit. It should be one of the first things you'll prepare to carry along on your bushcraft adventure indeed. Imagine your water bottle as a trusty sidekick, always by your side. Recognize the signs of dehydration, like a parched throat or some dizziness, and take them as secret signals from your body, telling you to take a water break.

Your water bottle is not just for quenching your thirst. It also prevents dehydration from messing up your adventure. Keep sipping from time to time, and you'll conquer the wild, staying as fresh as a morning breeze.

## THE COLD CONUNDRUM: DEFEATING HYPOTHERMIA

On the other side of excess heat is excess cold. Beware of this on your bushcraft adventure because if not properly anticipated and managed, excess cold can lead to hypothermia.

One way to prepare for and prevent hypothermia is by wearing different layers of cold-suitable clothing—dress in layers, just like a knight gearing up for a battle. The first layer is like a cozy hug, keeping you warm; the second layer is like a shield against the frosty wind, and the third layer is your magical cloak, resisting the moisture. Together, they create a force field against Hypothermia.

For times when the force of hypothermia becomes too strong for even your layered preventive clothing, the next thing to do is to battle the hypothermia. One essential thing to do is to recognize the early signs of hypothermia, like shivering or feeling extra clumsy. These are your secret alerts, prompting you to summon the warmth within your enchanted layers. Your body is like a furnace, producing heat to counter the cold spell.

Guess what? The American Red Cross is an excellent trove of resources for managing hypothermia and dehydration. It offers resources that will help you master the art of battling the elements. Dive into their wisdom to become the ultimate bushcraft adventurer!

Remember these guiding words in your quest to stay protected from the heat and cold while in the wild: Stay hydrated, dress wisely, and understand the signs. The bush is a wondrous realm, and with the right knowledge and preparation, every adventure becomes a triumph. So, young bushcrafters, armed with your water bottles, layers of enchanted clothing, and the wisdom of the American Red Cross, you're now ready to face the elements like true champions. Whether the sun blazes or the frost bites, you're equipped to dance with nature and emerge victorious in your bushcrafting adventures.

## PUTTING IT ALL TOGETHER: CREATING A KID-FRIENDLY FIRST AID KIT

Hey there, fearless adventurers! We're finally at the tail end of our learning process. Now, we want to prepare our first aid kit. Are you ready to unlock the secrets of your ultimate superhero tool—the Kid-Friendly First Aid Kit?

Imagine your first aid kit as a treasure chest filled with different items. What's inside, you ask? There are many things aimed to keep you protected and safe in your bushcrafting adventures and even every other day. For example, when we were learning about scrapes, we mentioned bandages. This is one of the items that will make up your first aid kit. Bandages are like trusty shields guarding against scrapes and cuts. We also have tweezers to banish splinters and tiny beasts from your kingdom and antiseptic wipes to cleanse and purify your wound. These antiseptic wipes take on the job of soap and water and even do it a lot better.

Many companies like Johnson & Johnson offer readymade first aid kits that you can purchase and take along on your bushcrafting exploration or adventure. But, if you're feeling in the mood for some DIY project, you can take on the challenge of assembling your very own custom first aid kit and tailoring it to your unique adventures.

## HOW-TO: DIY FIRST AID KIT

If you want to organize your first aid kit, here are some things you need to get done:

- **First Aid Bag**

Your first item will be the first aid bag. After all, this will be the housing for all your first aid items to keep them safe. When choosing a first aid bag for your bushcraft adventure, there are things you must look out for.

- **Waterproof**

Your first aid bag must be waterproof to shield its contents in situations where you come in contact with water. For example, you might fall into a large water body on your adventure, or you might encounter unexpected rain. In this situation, if your First aid bag isn't waterproof, it might render some of your items, like bandages, useless.

- **Puncture-Proof**

Your first aid bag must be sturdy. If you get a bag that isn't puncture-proof, imagine a situation where you mistakenly drag it against a pointed part of a tree or where it falls on a sharp object. If your first aid bag gets punctured, it may cause you to lose some of the content or even allow water into the bag and compromise the content.

- **Compact Size**

In your bushcraft adventure, you need a compact first aid kit for easy movement. You want your first aid kit to take only some available space. Instead, you need something compact enough for you to move around easily and also leave space for you to carry other necessary items for your exploration.

- **Easy to Organize**

Time is of the essence in emergencies. Your first aid bag should be a beacon of efficiency, with pockets and dividers ensuring swift access to crucial items when every second counts.

With your first aid bag selected, the next thing to do for your DIY First aid Kit is to select the items to include in your kit. So, let's look at some of these items, starting with

## TRAUMA ITEMS

Trauma items focus on significant injuries like knife cuts that could hinder movement or jeopardize your survival. Their focus is usually to stop excessive bleeding.

- **Sterile Heavy Gauze (Combine Dressings):** For applying pressure to wounds and restricting excess blood flow.
- **Roller Bandages:** Essential for holding a dressing in place or applying pressure to control bleeding.
- **Trauma Pads:** Large sterile pads for dressing deep wounds, often imbued with a blood-clotting agent.
- **Butterfly Closures:** Vital for closing large wounds.
- **Wound Stapler or Suture Kit:** While suturing is best left to medical professionals, in survival situations, a wound stapler might be a more accessible option.

- **Blood Clotting Agent:** Homeostatic agents to aid blood clotting and minimize blood loss.
- **Tourniquet:** A last resort, a bandana can double as a tourniquet, but use caution.
- **Burn Salve:** A must-have for treating burns, with petroleum jelly for minor burns and antiseptic burn salve for extensive burns.

## WOUND TREATMENT ITEMS

Once we have the trauma item lists sorted, we can now proceed to the next set of items. These are items for treating minor wounds like scrapes, bug bites, and so on.

- **Nitrile Gloves:** Many pairs for hygiene when treating wounds.
- **Tweezers:** Essential for removing debris from wounds.
- **Cotton Tip Swabs:** Useful for debris removal from wounds and eyes.
- **Magnifying Glass:** Handy for inspecting small debris or splinters.
- **60cc Syringe with Irrigation Tip:** For thorough wound cleaning.
- **Antiseptic Wipes:** Ensuring cleanliness when dealing with surface wounds.
- **Small Scissors:** For precision in cutting bandages.
- **Safety Pins:** Multi-purpose tools for removing splinters or securing bandages.
- **Antibiotic Ointment or Iodine:** Applied before dressing wounds for added protection.
- **Adhesive Bandages (Band-Aids):** Common aids for minor wounds.

- **Non-Adhesive Sterile Wound Dressings:** Lighter alternatives to gauze. It is used for controlling bleeding and wound cleaning.
- **Moleskin:** To protect your scrapes and blisters. You'll need a lot of this on your adventure.
- **Medical Tape:** Secures dressings and bandages in place.

BONE/LIGAMENT INJURIES ITEMS

There are times you might fracture yourself during your adventure. In such cases, you might need some items like;

- **Ace Bandage:** Essential for wrapping and supporting sprains.
- **Triangle Bandages:** Versatile sterile bandanas for various uses, from dressing wounds to creating slings.
- **Bendable Foam-Coated Splint:** A small, bendable aluminum-coated foam splint for versatile support.

MEDICATIONS: REMEDIES FOR AILMENTS

Include essential medications for allergies, insect bites, diarrhea, pain relief, antibiotics, EpiPen, anti-fungal cream, and potassium iodide for nuclear emergencies. Honey packets provide quick energy for treating hypothermia.

MISCELLANEOUS ITEMS: TOOLS FOR EVERY OCCASION

A flashlight ensures visibility during dark emergencies, and scissors or a knife aid in removing clothing around wounds. Sunscreen, lip ointment, and extra ziplock bags add versatility to your survival backpack.

Listen up, young bush crafters; while the first aid kit is yours, there are some items contained within that you must not use without adult supervision so as not to cause further harm to yourself.

Also, always remember this: Knowledge is Power. Regardless of how essential or well-packed your first aid kit is, it will only be useful if you know how to use the content. Every bandage, every wipe is a piece of your armor waiting to be unleashed. Learn about your tools, their strengths, and the situations they conquer. That is where the American Red Cross Society also comes into play. They offer different courses on emergency medical situations and how to provide help in such situations. On their website, you can learn how to assemble your first aid kit, how to use each item, and how to apply them when needed. Taking the courses offered by the American Red Cross is like leveling up in the game of healing—you become the ultimate healing champion and, consequently, a well-prepared and pro bush crafter.

Additionally, when going on your adventure, you can go with a first aid manual and flip through the pages when needed. It's not just a book; it's your guide on how to make effective use of a first aid kit. Know when and how to use each item, from cleansing a wound to banishing germs. The manual is your guide, transforming you from a novice into a First Aid Wizard.

## COMFORT IN THE MIDST OF AN ADVENTURE: STUFFED ANIMALS AND BOOKISH COMPANIONS

While your first aid kit is essential for your bushcrafting journey, you also need other items to add a bit of comfort and companionship to your rest breaks. This is where your comfort items come in. They are your loyal allies during times of distress.

For example, you can take with you on your journey a favorite stuffed animal, a fluffy guardian ready to absorb fears and provide cuddly courage. Or a book transporting you to far-off lands and calming the storm within. These items aren't just extras; they're secret weapons against stress and anxiety. A hug from your stuffed buddy or a dive into a captivating story can turn the tide in your favor.

Once you have everything set up, you're ready for your adventure. However, your preparation continues after packing your first aid kit. Instead, you must regularly check and replace expired or used items in their kit. Conduct regular audits like a seasoned explorer, ensuring your tools are ever-ready for the next epic adventure.

Remember, the Kid-Friendly First Aid Kit isn't just a box—it's your superhero utility belt, your secret weapon in conquering the unpredictable wilds of life. So, young champions, let the adventures begin.

# CONCLUSION

In the quest for your exploration of the wild, this book has opened up your knowledge base and filled you with directives and needed information like a treasure map leading to the heart of the wild. To help your bushcraft journey, we have covered many aspects along the way.

We started with the basics. To introduce you, our young explorer, to the common terminologies associated with bushcraft and introduce everything you'll learn in the course of the book. We stayed true to our original purpose throughout the book, and gradually, you became exposed to the different aspects of your bushcraft adventure.

In the first chapter, we learned about shelters. Their importance, different kinds of shelters for bushcrafters and explorers, and the origin of each of these shelters. The second chapter introduced us to navigation and bearings in the wild. Here, you learn how to find your way around the wild with the use of navigational tools like the compass.

The chapter on navigating the urban settlements equipped you with the skills to read city landscapes, decipher maps and navigate public spaces. The concrete jungle is no longer a maze but an open book waiting for your exploration. Safety and awareness have become your trusted companions, guiding you through the urban playground. From recognizing safe havens to understanding "stranger danger," you've embraced the principles of city safety.

We also explored foods in the wild. While you may want to enter the woods with some provisions of your own, there are times when you need to forage for food. Together, we unfolded the secrets of foraging for food in the wild, teaching you to identify resources in unexpected places. From water fountains to edible plants, you've become a savvy forager grounded in ethics and responsibility.

Insects, once tiny creatures, have transformed into protein powerhouses. You've explored the world of edible insects, learned how to prepare them, and understood the science behind consuming these tiny creatures. The natural world's treasures have become your playground. Understanding foraging is more than finding food; it's about recognizing edible plants, avoiding toxic ones, and becoming an environmentally conscious explorer. Foraging ethics and safety have become your guiding principles. You've embraced responsibility, understanding the delicate balance between taking what you need and preserving the environment.

Our dedication to survival in the wild also led us to explore the art of fire creation; together, we learned the importance of safety and understood the responsibility that comes with fire in the wilderness. Beyond that, you also learned how to ride the storm. Look at yourself now, little weather wizard. You can now recognize basic

## CONCLUSION

weather patterns, prepare for different conditions, and understand the importance of weather-resistant shelters. Safety during extreme weather is now second nature.

Band-Aids and bravery have become your tools for healing. Understanding first aid basics, treating minor injuries, dealing with bug bites and rashes, and preventing dehydration and hypothermia have transformed you into a first aid hero.

While the skills you've learned from this book are essential for your exploration of the wild, you will also find some of them useful in other aspects of your daily lives. They are lessons that transcend the wild. For example, from time to time, even within the city, you might find yourself applying your knowledge of first aid to emergencies.

As you stand on the threshold of your epic adventure, armed with knowledge, respect for nature, and a dash of bravery, remember that the wilderness is your canvas. So, explore wisely, and let the great adventure unfold.

# LEAVE A 1-CLICK REVIEW

I would be incredibly thankful if you take just
60-seconds to write a brief review on Amazon,
even if it's just a few sentences!

https://amazon.com/review/create-review?asin=1960188275

# ABOUT THE AUTHOR

Conrad Presley has an academic background in psychology and sociology that uniquely positions him to explore and explain the deep-rooted psychological and social factors that underpin this enduring conflict.

Presley's journey into the realms of psychology and sociology began with his fervent curiosity about human behavior and societal dynamics. This intellectual pursuit led him to get advanced degrees in both fields, equipping him with a nuanced perspective on the intricate interplay between individual psychology and societal structures.

Presley has been driven by a relentless quest to understand and explain the psychological undercurrents and social constructs that shape global conflicts. His expertise lies in dissecting complex political narratives and revealing the human emotions and societal pressures that often go unnoticed but play a crucial role in shaping historical events.

With this book, Conrad wanted to share the knowledge acquired over time while he shared and practice bushcrafting in the wild with his son. Sharing these experiences as parent/child are important to the development of strong children.

# BIBLIOGRAPHY

American Red Cross Training Services. (n.d.). *What is First Aid? | Understand First Aid | Red Cross*. Red Cross. https://www.redcross.org/take-a-class/first-aid/performing-first-aid/what-is-first-aid

Agrawal, S. (2023, September 8). *Wind direction Meaning: Significance and effect of wind direction*. A-Z Animals. https://a-z-animals.com/blog/wind-direction-meaning-unraveling-the-significance-and-effects-of-wind-directions/

*Articles*. (n.d.). https://www.cedars-sinai.org/health-library/diseases-and-conditions/d/dehydration.html

Aboriginal Culture. (n.d.). Housing and Shelters. https://www.aboriginalculture.com.au/housing-and-shelters/

Atlantic Survival Gear. (n.d.). Survival Shelter - Natural. https://atlanticsurvivalgear.com/survival-shelter-natural/

Australian Aboriginal Science. (2015, May 20). Australian Indigenous Tools & Shelter. https://aascf.wordpress.com/2015/05/20/australian-indigenous-tools-shelter/

At the Edge Mountaineering. (n.d.). Navigation Techniques: Compass Bearings. https://www.attheedgemountaineering.co.uk/post/navigation-techniques-compass-bearings

Britannica Kids. (n.d.). African Architecture. https://kids.britannica.com/students/article/African-architecture/606828

*Bystander CPR*. (n.d.). cpr.heart.org. https://cpr.heart.org/en/resources/bystander-cpr

BBC Travel. (2023, March 12). Why bushcraft is booming again. https://www.bbc.com/travel/article/20230312-why-bushcraft-is-booming-again

Cleaver, S. (2023, June 14). *64 of the Funnest Outside Activities for Kids*. We Are Teachers. https://www.weareteachers.com/outside-activities-for-kids/

*Cold weather safety for children: Preventing frostbite & hypothermia*. (n.d.). HealthyChildren.org. https://www.healthychildren.org/English/safety-prevention/at-play/Pages/Cold-Weather-Safety.aspx

Est Gear. (n.d.). The Importance of Safety and Creating a Survival Shelter. Est Gear Blog. https://estgear.com/blogs/blog/the-importance-of-safety-and-creating-a-survival-shelter

European Civil Protection and Humanitarian Aid Operations. (n.d.). Shelter and

# BIBLIOGRAPHY

Settlements. https://civil-protection-humanitarian-aid.ec.europa.eu/what/humanitarian-aid/shelter-and-settlements en

EcoParent. (n.d.). *Build an Outdoor Play Shelter with Materials from Nature. EcoParent.* https://ecoparent.ca/eco-parenting/build-outdoor-play-shelter-materials-nature

*Edible plants: 7 plants you can actually eat in the wild.* (n.d.). Mossy Oak. https://www.mossyoak.com/edible-plants

*Fire safety in dry woodlands. . . - Pioneer Bushcraft.* (2019, May 30). Pioneer Bushcraft. https://www.pioneerbushcraft.org/fire-safety-in-dry-woodlands/

*Fire and cooking — woodland bushcraft.* (n.d.). Woodland Bushcraft. https://www.woodlandbushcraft.com/fireandcooking

*Family Bushcraft: Playing with Fire - Woodland Classroom.* (2020, March 4). Woodland Classroom. https://woodlandclassroom.com/event/family-bushcraft-playing-with-fire/

*Hypothermia.* (2020, January 24). Johns Hopkins Medicine. https://www.hopkinsmedicine.org/health/conditions-and-diseases/hypothermia

Heinnie Haynes. (n.d.). 14 Bushcraft Essentials. https://heinnie.com/blog/14-bushcraft-essentials/

Heinnie Haynes. (n.d.). 14 Bushcraft Essentials. https://heinnie.com/blog/14-bushcraft-essentials/

*How to dress your kids for the outdoors.* (n.d.). REI. https://www.rei.com/learn/expert-advice/how-to-dress-your-kids-for-the-outdoors.html

Herker, C. (2019, January 7). *Leave No Trace Principles for Kids — ScouterLife.* ScouterLife. https://www.scouterlife.com/blog/2016/5/11/leave-no-trace-principles-for-kids

*How to read wind direction. Even if it sounds too simple - Windy.app.* (n.d.). WINDY.APP. https://windy.app/blog/what-is-wind-direction.html

Harbour, S. (2023, March 12). *Foraging with Kids: 5 Easy-to-Find Wild Edibles.* An off Grid Life. https://www.anoffgridlife.com/foraging-with-kids

John. (2022, September 23). *Bushcraft fire skills.* Dorset Bushcraft Courses | Wildway Bushcraft. https://www.wildwaybushcraft.co.uk/bushcraft-fire

Jones, C. (2022, June 21). *Bushcraft First Aid – Top 5 issues you may need to deal with.* First Aid Training Co-operative. https://firstaidtrainingcooperative.co.uk/bushcraft-first-aid/

Jones, B. (2018, August 3). *A beginner's guide to finding wild edible plants that won't kill you.* Popular Science. https://www.popsci.com/find-wild-edible-plants/

Khan Academy. (n.d.). Foraging. Big History Project. https://www.khanacademy.org/humanities/big-history-project/early-humans/how-did-first-humans-live/a/foraging

# BIBLIOGRAPHY

*Learn edible wild plants here!* (n.d.). https://www.twineagles.org/edible-wild-plants.html

Kendall, J. (2020, March 4). *My Bushcraft Journal: Part #1 Building Better Shelters - Woodland Classroom.* Woodland Classroom. https://woodlandclassroom.com/my-bushcraft-journal-part-1-building-better-shelters/

McCoy, D. (2022, December 28). 25 Survival Skills For Kids • The Rustic Elk. *The Rustic Elk.* https://www.therusticelk.com/25-survival-skills-for-kids/

Much Better Adventures. (n.d.). Bushcraft: A Beginner's Guide. https://www.muchbetteradventures.com/magazine/bushcraft-a-beginners-guide/

Madden, K. (2023, August 29). *Public spaces where kids thrive: The places that work for kids work for everybody.* Social Life Project. https://www.sociallifeproject.org/public-spaces-where-kids-thrive/

Ovenden, S. (2023, August 8). *Foraging: A beginner's guide.* BBC Good Food. https://www.bbcgoodfood.com/howto/guide/foraging

*Poison ivy rash - Symptoms and causes - Mayo Clinic.* (2023, August 11). Mayo Clinic. https://www.mayoclinic.org/diseases-conditions/poison-ivy/symptoms-causes/syc-20376485

Pioneer Bushcraft. (2020). Make a Strong Connection to Nature in 2020. https://www.pioneerbushcraft.org/make-a-strong-connection-to-nature-in-2020/

Parker, L. (2022, March 19). Learning to Build Shelters and Fires with Kids. My Simple Wild. https://mysimplewild.com/2022/03/19/learning-to-build-shelters-and-fires-with-kids/

Princeton University Outdoor Action. (n.d.). Map & Compass Navigation. https://www.princeton.edu/~oa/manual/mapcompass3.shtml

Quora. (n.d.). What are some ways to find your way home after getting lost during a hike or camping trip. https://www.quora.com/What-are-some-ways-to-find-your-way-home-after-getting-lost-during-a-hike-or-camping-trip

*Quick and easy winter shelter for kids to build.* (n.d.). The Great Outdoors Stack Exchange. https://outdoors.stackexchange.com/questions/17436/quick-and-easy-winter-shelter-for-kids-to-build

RedCrossNW, V. a. P. B. (2020, September 24). *Teaching children how to make emergency calls.* American Red Cross NW Region. https://redcrossnw.org/2020/09/25/teaching-children-how-to-make-emergency-calls/

Rd, J. K. M. (2021, June 3). *What is foraging, and how do you get started?* Healthline. https://www.healthline.com/nutrition/foraging-for-food

*Rashes (Children).* (2011, September 6). WebMD. https://www.webmd.com/first-aid/rashes-children

Survival Stoic. (n.d.). Bushcraft Skills: The Ultimate Guide to Mastering the Wilderness. https://survivalstoic.com/bushcraft-skills/

# BIBLIOGRAPHY

Stanley. (n.d.). How to Stay Safe Outdoors and Recreate Responsibly. https://www.stanley1913.com/blogs/how-to-guides/how-to-stay-safe-outdoors-and-recreate-responsibly

*Survival Shelters | Yost Survival skills | Bushcraft and outdoor skills*. (2023, June 5). Survival Skills and Bushcraft for the Modern Survivalist. https://yostsurvivalskills.com/survival-shelters/#:~:text=Simply%20piling%20up%20enough%20leaves,bark%20slabs%20on%20dead%20trees.

Schunko, C., Wild, A., & Brandner, A. (2021). Exploring and limiting the ecological impacts of urban wild food foraging in Vienna, Austria. *Urban Forestry & Urban Greening*, *62*, 127164. https://doi.org/10.1016/j.ufug.2021.127164

Seattle YMCA. (n.d.). How to Use a Compass. https://www.seattleymca.org/blog/how-use-compass

Survival and Bushcrafts. (n.d.). Gunyah - The Australian Shelter. https://www.survivalandbushcrafts.com/gunyah-the-australian-shelter/

Snow, T. (2020, December 22). *Know hypothermia dangers*. Richland Health. https://richlandhealth.org/blog/2020/12/22/know-hypothermia-dangers/

The importance of fire in wilderness living. (2022, February 28). *Bushgear*. https://www.bushgear.co.uk/blogs/bush-telegraph-2017/the-importance-of-fire-in-wilderness-living

Twinkl. (n.d.). Native American Homes. https://www.twinkl.com.ng/teaching-wiki/native-american-homes

Taylor, C. (2023, October 25). *What is a wind direction instrument, and how does it work? - Maximum weather instruments*. Maximum Weather Instruments. https://www.maximum-inc.com/learning-center/what-are-wind-speed-direction-instruments-and-how-do-they-work/#:~:text=Wind%20direction%20matters%20because%20it,also%20important%20for%20military%20use.

*Urban Foraging: Pick wild berries in local green spaces*. (n.d.). ParentMap. https://www.parentmap.com/article/summer-urban-foraging-pick-wild-berries-in-local-parks

Wikihow. (n.d.). How to Build a Natural Shelter in the Jungle. https://www.wikihow.com/Build-a-Natural-Shelter-in-the-Jungle

Willis, D. (n.d.). What is Bushcraft? David Willis - Bushcraft & Wilderness Living Skills. http://www.davidwillis.info/what-is-bushcraft/

Wikihow. (n.d.). How to Use a Compass. https://www.wikihow.com/Use-a-Compass

Wikipedia. (n.d.). Wigwam. https://en.wikipedia.org/wiki/Wigwam

Wilderchild. (2022, March 2). *A beginner's guide to foraging for wild edibles with kids*. Wilder Child - Nature-Connected Parenting. https://wilderchild.com/blogs/news/foraging-for-wild-edibles-with-kids

# BIBLIOGRAPHY

Wowak, D. (2023, August 11). *First aid kits A to Z*. Coalcracker Bushcraft. https://coalcrackerbushcraft.com/blogs/journal/first-aid-kits-a-to-z

Wildernessarena. (2023, July 12). How to build shelters in the wild. - Geek slop. Geek Slop. https://www.geekslop.com/life/survival/food-water-shelter/2012/building-shelters-in-the-wild

Morton, C. (2023, December 8). Bushcraft 101: How to build a survival shelter in the wilderness. Mortons on the Move. https://www.mortonsonthemove.com/survival-shelter/

Edwards, D. (2023, March 19). How to build a survival shelter when lost on a hike. Trail Hiking Australia. https://www.trailhiking.com.au/safety/how-to-build-a-survival-shelter/

Basics of wilderness survival shelters. (n.d.). Alderleaf Wilderness College. https://www.wildernesscollege.com/wilderness-survival-shelters.html

Arro, K. M. (2022, September 15). The importance of bystander CPR - First Aid pro Adelaide. First Aid Pro Adelaide. https://www.firstaidproadelaide.com.au/blog/the-importance-of-bystander-cpr/

American Red Cross Training Services. (n.d.-a). CPR Steps | Perform CPR | Red Cross. Red Cross. https://www.redcross.org/take-a-class/cpr/performing-cpr/cpr-steps

Bystander CPR. (n.d.-b). cpr.heart.org. https://cpr.heart.org/en/resources/bystander-cpr

Felman, A. (2018, June 26). First aid, the recovery position, and CPR. https://www.medicalnewstoday.com/articles/153849#cardio-pulmonary-resuscitation-cpr

Made in the USA
Las Vegas, NV
26 February 2025

18747824R00095